Psychoanalytic Parent-Infant Psychotherapy and Mentalization

T0386195

This book is an account of best practice in psychoanalytic parent-infant psychotherapy (PPIP) and mentalizing, bringing the two approaches in dialogue in relation to infancy.

While being similar, PPIP and mentalizing emphasize different aspects of interpersonal processes and apply different ways of intervening. In this text, chapters detail how the models are put into practice, describing the different settings in which they are applied, and the research that has been undertaken to shape them. Exploring the ideas and practice of both approaches, including how they may complement each other and where differing stances may be adopted in relation to clinical material and therapy, this volume enriches the range of ways of working available to the clinician.

Psychoanalytic Parent-Infant Psychotherapy and Mentalization provides an overview of the practices of PPIP and mentalization for professionals, but also for anyone interested in understanding the model of psychotherapy and the ideas behind it.

Tessa Baradon is trained in child psychotherapy and psychoanalysis. She led the development of the model psychoanalytic parent-infant psychotherapy which has been implemented in different socio-economic and cultural settings internationally. She has published widely on the topic.

Dr Chloe Campbell is Deputy Director of the Psychoanalysis Unit. Her research interests include mentalizing, epistemic trust and attachment theory.

Psychoanalytic Parent-Infant Psychotherapy and Mentalization

A Dialogue in Theory and Practice

Tessa Baradon and Chloe Campbell

LONDON AND NEW YORK

Cover image: private collection of authors

First published 2023
by Routledge
4 Park Square, Milton Park, Abingdon, Oxon OX14 4RN

and by Routledge
605 Third Avenue, New York, NY 10158

Routledge is an imprint of the Taylor & Francis Group, an informa business

© 2023 Tessa Baradon and Chloe Campbell

British Library Cataloguing-in-Publication Data
A catalogue record for this book is available from the British Library

Library of Congress Cataloging-in-Publication Data
Names: Baradon, Tessa, author.
Title: Psychoanalytic parent-infant psychotherapy and
    mentalization : a dialogue in theory and practice / Tessa Baradon
    and Chloe Campbell.
Description: Abingdon, Oxon ; New York, NY : Routledge,
    2023. | Includes bibliographical references and index.
Identifiers: LCCN 2022021982 (print) | LCCN 2022021983
    (ebook) | ISBN 9780367904296 (hbk) | ISBN 9780367904289
    (pbk) | ISBN 9781003024323 (ebk)
Subjects: LCSH: Parent-infant psychotherapy. | Parent and infant. |
    Mentalization Based Therapy.
Classification: LCC RJ502.5 .B373 2023 (print) | LCC RJ502.5
    (ebook) | DDC 618.92/8914—dc23/eng/20220625
LC record available at https://lccn.loc.gov/2022021982
LC ebook record available at https://lccn.loc.gov/2022021983

ISBN: 978-0-367-90429-6 (hbk)
ISBN: 978-0-367-90428-9 (pbk)
ISBN: 978-1-003-02432-3 (ebk)

DOI: 10.4324/9781003024323

Typeset in Bembo
by Apex CoVantage, LLC

Contents

Foreword

Peter Fonagy

OBE, *Professor of Contemporary Psychoanalysis and Developmental Science,*
Head of Division for Psychology and Language Sciences, UCL;
Chief Executive of the Anna Freud Centre

This book forms an innovative conversation between two ways of thinking and working – psychoanalytic parent-infant psychotherapy and mentalization – that have much in common: shared influences, histories and traditions and perhaps most emphatically, a shared interest in thinking about how minds meet other minds and impact on each other. Nevertheless, as mentalizing grew as an offshoot of psychoanalysis, it developed different priorities and concerned itself relatively little with the theoretical body of ideas from which its inspiration originally drew its strengths. By the same token, the psychoanalytic community mostly tended to ignore mentalizing theory as just one of the many clinical outgrowths over its century of history, that drew on its conceptual richness, perhaps shined brightly for a brief moment, only to fizzle out and be forgotten by most once its Andy Warhol 15 minutes of fame had passed. So psychoanalysis and mentalizing have been in peaceful coexistence for the past decade with few overt efforts to make links and connections.

Two key contributors to these traditions have undertaken a joint project to address this regrettable separation. They provided a wonderful opportunity not just to explore the differences or similarities of understanding, but far more deeply to examine the dialectic between the rich psychoanalytic focus on unconscious concerns of the parent and the baby and the admittedly narrower and neuroscientifically bounded concerns of the mentalizing model with the phenomenology of parenting. The result, as the reader will be able to judge, is a significant step forward for both orientations, especially the mentalizing perspective.

There are two fundamental psychological constructions about carer-infant relations that can be brought to clinical and scientific study (Fonagy, Moran, Edgcumbe, Kennedy, & Target, 1993). What questions, or questions of content, explore the content of the experience of two minds exploring each other's thoughts and feelings. The how questions, or questions of process, concern mental mechanisms that generate content under clinical scrutiny in PPIP and other psychodynamic clinical encounters.

Mental representations and mental processes are as interdependent as a symphony and an orchestra or, more modestly, the tune and the violin that generates the sound.

Understandably, psychoanalytic clinicians have traditionally been more involved with the what questions and were less concerned with constraints that mechanisms of cognition could impose on superabundant thinking about the complexity of conflicting emotions and ideas that may be needed to explain the clinical experience. As a consequence, notwithstanding the progress in social and neuroscience, psychoanalysis remains the richest body of understanding of human behaviour available to us today. It is a joy to teach the development of psychoanalytic ideas because of the extraordinary insightfulness and creativity of accounts it offers of commonly and less commonly encountered human experience. Clinicians reach into this treasure trove of narratives of clinical encounters and find similarities to past cases and suppositions that serve as guides not just to understanding but also to conduct – what to say.

Mentalizing theory has taken a different route and tries as best it can to provide accounts of similar phenomena in terms of assumed limitations of mental process and find patterns of mechanistic dysfunction which may provide a plausible explanation. As a theory, it is almost barren of content, and as a therapy, it gives few suggestions to clinicians about what to expect as common concerns of types of patients. It gives advice on how to work clinically (well to be truthful, it says more about how not to work) and focuses on ways to enhance the patient's capacity to accurately and without distortion process their experience of the world.

But the world of early years has always been slightly different. Because psychoanalytic clinicians working with infants, especially those working from a developmental Anna Freudian perspective, observed the maturational progression and the emergence of the human mind in vivo in the course of consultation, their theorizing tended to be more modest and constrained. Nevertheless, it retained the richness of its psychoanalytic origins. Mentalizing, with its roots in attachment theory, has mapped only a small part of the interaction of carer and infant although it brought a sharp perspective primarily through the work of one of the originators of the mentalizing approach George Gergely (2007). So infant-carer work is perhaps the ideal ground on which a reconciliation of the mentalizing and psychoanalytic approaches can be sought. And Baradon and Campbell's book takes exceptionally good advantage of this potential. By placing the approaches side by side, they are able to draw from each to facilitate understanding of the clinical situation and through that manage to enrich both approaches to the advantage of the thousands of clinicians who may benefit from reading this book. The book is remarkably well structured to achieve its declared aim of enabling practitioners to create an optimally effective approach to help babies and carers with the challenges of bringing a new human mind into the social world with the greatest potential and enable parents to support this process of growth drawing on their immense natural propensity to do so. This is a positive book, committed not to highlighting limitations but identifying opportunities for growth – as indeed a book about infant development should be.

There is a particular area where Baradon and Campbell find exceptionally fertile and for me deeply satisfying common ground for mutual enrichment. There is an old proverb, a cliché almost now, that it "takes a village to raise a child". It is a trope that repetition derives from our folk understanding that the mundane yet extraordinary task of supporting the growth of new minds is a challenging and collective responsibility. Its resonance is a response to those aspects of modern life that make the work of thinking about mental states in a compassionate and responsive way more challenging than ever: isolation, competition, diminishing social and ecological security and an ever-more complex and demanding cultural and economic environment can all work against the reflective generosity of support that new babies and new parents need. An often-repeated criticism of attachment thinking and traditional psychoanalytic approaches to thinking about the earliest social relationships is that they emphasize the role of the dyad at the expense of thinking about the significance of the wider network of social relationships around the infant and parent. Both PPIP and mentalizing share a growing awareness that the relative social isolation in which modern parents engage in caregiving makes it much harder to access another trusted person/mind to help think about stressful situations in order to regulate affect and regain balanced mentalizing. PPIP for vulnerable parents has always worked because it taps into a universal need that we all have to access other minds to help us restore our own capacity to think and to self-regulate. The dialogue in this book seeks to develop new ways of thinking about how both mentalizing theory and PPIP can develop in the future to together create a culture of understanding minds around babies and parents to support them in creating an experience of one another as a source of consolation, safety and joy.

References

Fonagy, P., Moran, G. S., Edgcumbe, R., Kennedy, H., & Target M. (1993). The roles of mental representations and mental processes in therapeutic action. *Psychoanal Study Child*, *48*, 9–48.

Gergely, G. (2007). The social construction of the subjective self: The role of affect-mirroring, markedness, and ostensive communication in self development. In L. Mayes, P. Fonagy, & M. Target (Eds.), *Developmental science and psychoanalysis: Integration and inovation* (pp. 45–82). London, UK: Karnac Books.

1 Introduction

This book came into being out of in-passing conversations in the corridors and over the kettle at the Anna Freud Centre (AFC), when it was a psychoanalytic institution and at the same time developing mentalizing theory and practice in relation to children. We, Tessa Baradon, representing psychoanalytic parent-infant psychotherapy, and Chloe Campbell, coming from a mentalizing perspective, came up against differences between the two forms of working, while also sharing a keen interest in how minds meet other minds, and in particular how parents and infants impact each other. The key objective of this book is to continue this dialogue between psychoanalytic parent-infant psychotherapy (PPIP) and mentalizing, both influential approaches in the repertoire of therapies available to families with young children. The practices of both PPIP and mentalizing, as therapeutic modalities, are underpinned by relational models of personality development, structure and functioning. Differences in emphasis between the models, for example, in the extent to which early relational experiences shadow current interactions, are related to different emphases in practice. We hope to cast some light on these differences, but also, by discussing them alongside each other, explore how they may provide the clinician in both modalities with a richer and more diverse range of ideas to inform their work with different patients. Although we talk across the book in terms of the therapist as the practitioner, we believe that the ideas we set out here are relevant to all practitioners in the field, as the complexity of the postnatal period will face anyone working with the emotional ties between babies and their parents.

About PPIP

Psychoanalytic parent-infant psychotherapy is a treatment modality that addresses difficulties and disturbances in the parent-infant relationship that threaten the healthy development of the infant. The modality is

DOI: 10.4324/9781003024323-1

informed by psychoanalytic and attachment ideas and by cross-disciplinary research about relational environments that support infant development and those that negatively impact development. Its underpinning framework of development and psychopathology is psychoanalytic in the Anna Freudian tradition (see Chapter 4).

A core competency in infant mental health is the ability to hold both parent/parents and infant in mind:

> to maintain the perspective not only of the parent but also that of the baby. . . . To maintain a focus on the parent-infant relationship as a dynamic system, and . . . to apply interventions flexibly in-line with the strengths, vulnerabilities and wider social context of each infant, parent and family.
> (The Association for Infant Mental Health UK, 2019, p. 5)

In PPIP this view is taken a step further: both the parent/parents and the infant are seen as recipients of the therapy. In other words, the infant is a co-patient in PPIP, and their developmental needs, capacities, anxieties and defences are addressed directly. In turn, parents are helped to become aware of their feelings and behaviours and thoughts about their baby, understand their difficulties and strengths as parents, be curious about the sources of these, and consider the impact on their baby. Some of the sources may be known to the parent ("I get really impatient when I haven't had a good night's sleep"). Other thoughts and feelings that drive behaviour may lie outside the parent's awareness, or consciousness.

One of the fundamental ideas that underpins any psychoanalytic approach is that we are all influenced by unconscious thoughts and beliefs that shape how we think, feel, behave and relate to other people. Unconscious thinking is itself shaped by the experiences we had when we were young, how we were parented and how our view of ourselves and the world was made by our own feelings and thoughts as they bumped into other people's. Experiences are then recast and elaborated by fantasy life, imagination, desire and other internal elements of our minds. PPIP encompasses the psychoanalytic model of development which places emphasis on unconscious mental processes in the parent and between parent and infant: those processes that are denied access to consciousness because of their painful or conflictual content, as well as the earliest non conscious processes that are associated with procedural memory. The unconscious internal world of the parent is central to understanding the relational environment that the baby inhabits.

Both unconscious (thoughts and feelings that are rendered outside of awareness because of their painful and conflictual nature) and non-conscious (earliest procedural/automatic knowledge) are expressed primarily in embodied language. To this end, PPIP pays attention to non-verbal aspects of communication of parent, baby and between them. Close attention to the baby's communications helps the baby organize his or her experience and build a sense of self.

About mentalizing

Mentalizing is defined as the imaginative process of trying to understand the mental states (the thoughts, feelings, beliefs, knowledge and ideas) that drive our own and other people's behaviours, responses and expressions. Mentalizing is both a theoretical approach and a form of psychotherapeutic practice – also partly derived from psychoanalytic ideas – that seeks to understand and treat mental health disorder and improve social functioning by supporting the capacity to mentalize both the self and others. Mentalization theory, like PPIP, assumes unconscious activity, but in practice, holds that idea lightly. The focus of mentalizing practice is on the thoughts and feelings that shape behaviour, irrespective of their source. The approach we take to mentalizing in this book is shaped by the fundamental principle of PPIP work: that the baby's experiences and his/her communications about his/her experiences are central to theory and practice. We seek to integrate this infant-led perspective with mentalizing, while also considering the particular mentalizing challenges and tasks involved in parenting a very young child (see Chapter 5).

The mentalizing literature has tended to focus on what happens when adults and older children are unable to reflect on, and so regulate, their states; in this book we are trying to translate the impact of mentalizing difficulties on infants and parents and their relationships. We will describe processes that render the state of disarray we think an infant experiences when his or her parent is persistently unable to mentalize him or her or constantly misattributes mental states. We will also elaborate some of the processes that may get in the way of the parent being able to accurately recognize and acknowledge their infant as an infant, with age-appropriate needs and physio-emotional states.

Mentalization-based approaches for parents of infants have been developed to enhance parents' capacity for reflective functioning, in particular in relation to their babies (Minding the Baby (Sadler et al., 2013; Slade et al., 2019), MBT-Parenting (Keaveny et al., 2012; Midgley & Vrouva, 2012), the Lighthouse programme (Byrne et al., 2019), Mothering from the Inside Out (Suchman, 2016; Suchman et al., 2020, 2017)). This is very much in line with the developmental model of how mentalizing is acquired through the experience of being mentalized

(Luyten, Campbell, Allison, & Fonagy, 2020). Influenced by PPIP's emphatic interest in the baby's perspective, agency and its influence on the parent, in this book, we have shifted to viewing the relational world of parent and baby as a "mentalizing system" in its own right. The key idea presented is that early infancy presents a particular problem to the parent, in as much as developmentally the infant's contribution to the mentalizing system is via bodily-based communication of engagement with and interest in their parent. For example, in the Still Face experiment (Tronick, Als, Adamson, Wise, & Brazelton, 1978), the baby's initial response to the parent's presentation of a still face is to try to re-establish reciprocity. We can regard these behaviours, which aim to call the parent back from the still face retreat, as cues to the parent to "think about me, your baby" – that is, to re-establish their mentalizing capacities that underpinned the pleasurable interaction. At the same time, the baby's agency is, of course, limited and an infant cannot, beyond attempts as described, contribute to the stabilization of the parent's mentalizing capacity when this is lowered. In fact, because of the infant's raw emotional states and the intensity and immediacy of its calls on the parent and their attachment system, the infant often can be seen as a highly arousing non-mentalizing partner in this mentalizing system when it is, whether temporarily or consistently, not functioning adequately. This thinking, which validates infant sentience and also recognizes the limits to it within the parent-infant mentalizing system, will be discussed and illustrated across the book.

This conceptualization of mentalizing-informed therapy could inform the development of a new modality within the repertoire of mentalizing interventions, one in which an *embodied dialogue* between parent and baby would be central.

Influences on PPIP and mentalizing

Stern has argued that specific therapeutic modalities are developed in response to need:

> the history of psychotherapy is, in large part, the story of encounters between existent therapeutic approaches and new clinical populations for whom the existing concepts and techniques were not designed. The specific psychopathology that is clinically addressed is of crucial importance to an understanding of the therapeutic approach that develops. Theories arise with specific clinical phenomena in mind.
>
> (Stern, 1995, p. 1)

PPIP was developed in response to a need identified in infants, as a specific category of childhood. MBT was, similarly, developed in response to an awareness and concern that a particular patient group – individuals with a diagnosis of BPD – were not receiving effective help.

In addition to psychoanalytic ideas, attachment theory and research have influenced both PPIP and mentalizing work. In PPIP, attachment has operationalized ideas about good enough (Winnicott, 1953), mid-range sensitive parenting (Beebe et al., 2000; Beebe & Steele, 2013) and helped in delineating the kinds of parental states of mind and behaviours that support infant development, and those that are associated with disorganized attachment in the young child (Madigan et al., 2006). Attachment research has also highlighted transgenerational mechanisms of trauma that contribute to relational difficulties between parent and infant (Steele, Perez, Segal, & Steele, 2016) (Fonagy, Steele, & Steele, 1991). The work of Daniel Stern in particular has opened the way to studying the experiences of the baby in terms of their attachment relationships (Stern, 1985). Attachment theory has also been central to mentalizing work; the relationship between parental reflective function (mentalizing capacity) and infant attachment security was explored in some of the earliest research in this area (Fonagy, Steele, Moran, Steele, & Higgitt, 1993), and it is an association that has proved robust (Luyten et al., 2020). In particular, mentalizing as a protective factor against the detrimental impact of relational trauma points to therapeutic approaches that mediate parental impingements by enhancing their capacities to "see" the baby before them (the "baby in arms" as opposed to the "baby in mind") and reflect on the baby's experience (Ensink, Begin, Normandin, & Fonagy, 2017).

Both PPIP and mentalizing theory have also learnt from the rapid expansion of neurobiology and developmental science that has taken place in the last twenty years or so. Practice has been transformed by our understanding of how the brain develops in utero and postnatally, and how environment and genes interact to move each infant along their particular developmental trajectory. Specifically to PPIP, an understanding of the impact of cumulative, overwhelming stress – toxic stress – on the brain and metabolic systems, and a sense of urgency in terms of the infant's developmental time-table and windows of opportunity, informs the therapeutic approach. PPIP canvasses for early referral of infants and their parents, and prioritizes reducing toxic interactions as much as supporting growth-promoting relational environments. In terms of mentalizing, a growing understanding of the relatively distinct underlying neural circuits that underpin social cognition has helped to clarify that mentalizing is not a unidimensional process – rather there are different domains of mentalizing and we all have varying strengths and weaknesses in these domains that make up our individual mentalizing profile. Similarly, a growing appreciation of the slow and sometimes uneven emergence of full mentalizing capacities across childhood and adolescence has helped us understand expectable developmental trajectories (Malle, 2021).

The fact that PPIP and mentalizing have adapted and been influenced by different ideas and emerging research findings is in itself a reflection of the models, which both seek to be open-minded, patient-led and pragmatic when it comes to meeting the needs of adults, children, infants and their families. Shared pragmatism is illustrated in the recognition that individuals who present with curtailed mental functioning require interventions that support this development before they can make use of more interpretive, classical therapy. Fonagy, Moran and colleagues suggested that

> psychoanalytic treatment [authors' comment: of individuals with inhibited mental processes] frequently reveals early experiences of having been overwhelmed by affect (theirs and their object's) at a time when the capacity to bar from access to consciousness specific affect-laden representation was not available.
>
> (Fonagy, Moran, Edgcumbe, Kennedy, & Target, 1993, p. 26)

This account describes some of the patients diagnosed with borderline personality disorder, for whom mentalizing programmes were initially developed, and some of the traumatized parents who attend PPIP. The deficits in mental process are characterized by impaired differentiation between external and internal worlds, by difficulties in linking cause and effect and predicting, and in a lack of understanding of, and sometimes even words for, affects. Anna Freud coined the term "developmental therapy" (Hurry, 1998) for therapeutic techniques that cultivate the emergence of these processes. Alvarez, too, argues that we need to adapt therapeutic activity to build the foundations of mental functioning in children who are profoundly impaired in their thinking (Alvarez, 2010). Fonagy and Bateman expanded this view to the theory and practice of mentalization: "In an attempt to cope, the individual decouples the mind from others' minds and relies on earlier psychological mechanisms to organize the experience and in doing so reveals fragments of the self" (Fonagy & Bateman, 2006, p. 414). It is worth noting that infancy by its very nature involves building the mind and therefore what happens in the parent–infant relationship is a model, in some ways, for the provision of developmental help via psychotherapy.

A baby's world from a PPIP and mentalizing perspective

The richly different cultural and social worlds that humans have evolved in response to their circumstances means that there is no single way to parent, as the anthropologist Hrdy has so cogently argued (Hrdy, 2011). And of course, there is no single way to be a baby: a newborn has to be ready to adapt to the many possible templates of human experience. Perhaps this is why young babies seem so enigmatic: that slightly watchful, mysterious presence of an absolutely brand-new baby reflects how they are waiting to see what kind of world is about to open up, or be unleashed, and how to be in it. Babies are a kind of vestigial shortcut to our evolutionary past: they reveal our basic requirements in their rawest forms, in which physical and emotional urges are merged in the need to survive and learn more about how to be a human.

The dialogue of this book comes out of a shared fascination with the worlds of babies, but also the understanding that the parental work of initiating a baby into the world, especially a turbulent world, can be hard. Both psychoanalysis and evolutionarily informed mentalizing theory have recognized that the intensive demands of raising an infant can create conflict between parent and baby. For a parent who feels isolated or threatened or at a loss in relation to the task of caring, the work can be harder, the risk of conflictual feelings greater and the emotional and physical toll potentially higher. Both mentalizing and PPIP seek to provide both parent and infant with an experience of a world in which their mental states and needs can be tolerated, supported and indeed appreciated. The hope is that some of this experience is carried forward in the infant and the parent's experience of each other, and colours the infant's understanding of the way the world that he or she has been born into.

Structure of the book

This book contains both theoretical and practical elements. In the initial four chapters, we set out our theoretical framework of infant development and trauma in the parent-infant context and introduce PPIP and mentalizing.

In Chapter 2, we explain some of the key ideas about infant mental health that have informed and shaped PPIP: the thinking of psychoanalysts such as Bion and Winnicott, attachment theory and mentalizing, and the work of major developmental researchers such as Stern, Beebe and Tronick. We also consider the role of fathers and other aspects of and variations in family structures and their bearing on PPIP, particularly as it has evolved in recent years, and describe a growing interest in and emphasis on the wider "social ecology" and its impact on the parent-infant relationship and clinical thinking about the role of culture in parenting.

In Chapter 3, we cover thinking about trauma in the parent-infant relationship: how trauma might be transmitted across generations, and how infants adapt to and defend against relational trauma in their early experiences. Much of this communication between infants, parents and practitioners will be embodied and occur too rapidly to be consciously registered. Recognizing and making sense of fleeting but potent embodied communication requires particular understanding and self-awareness, as we explain in Chapters 3 and 4.

In Chapter 4, we describe the PPIP model as it was developed at the AFC and how it has taken the thinking on development and trauma discussed in Chapters 2 and 3, and created the theoretical framework for PPIP work. The legacy of Anna Freud's thinking on the model is traced, and the ways in which PPIP has more recently evolved in response to social change, cultural shifts and developing knowledge about infant mental health.

Chapter 5 explains mentalizing theory in more detail and explores some of the ideas in relation to infancy and to PPIP. Some of the key concepts in mentalizing are set out and we work to apply them to thinking about the particular demands and developmental tasks faced by both new babies and new parents. We explain the concept of epistemic trust and how the mentalizing stance – one of the key concepts in mentalization-based treatments – can be brought to help infants develop their emerging sense of self.

In Chapter 6 we describe the practice of PPIP, bringing in a mentalizing perspective. Since a specific mentalizing-based PIP programme does not exist, we are limited to a mentalizing commentary on PPIP. We cover practicalities such as settings and how the work itself takes place but also use vignettes and descriptions of clinical issues to bring to life some of the theory described in the earlier chapters, drawing on moments when mentalizing ideas can really come into dialogue with PPIP and make particular contributions to parent-infant interactions.

Chapter 7 uses an example of a microanalysis of a PPIP case, in which moment-to-moment interactions between parent, infant and therapist are studied at a micro-level to reveal embodied, fleeting and unconscious processes which shape and build the nature of a relationship. The purpose of this chapter is to demonstrate how some of the processes theorized in Chapters 2–5 correspond to the bread and butter of human relational experiences. The chapter is based on an earlier publication, but has been reworked with an additional mentalizing perspective.

Chapter 8 describes how PPIP has been adapted to working in community settings, picking up on some of the ideas discussed in Chapters 2 and 5 about the role of the social environment around parents and infants in supporting the earliest stages of their relationship. A case example is given of a community-based PPIP programme, New Beginnings (Baradon, 2013; Baradon et al., 2017; Sleed, Baradon, & Fonagy, 2013), in which ideas drawn from mentalizing have been important influence.

In Chapter 9 we think about therapists and practitioners working with babies and their parents. We describe what is expected of someone who takes on the challenging but extraordinarily satisfying work of supporting the mental health of infants and their parents as they go through two of the most vulnerable, and critical, stages of human experience: the struggle to survive and grow a sense of self in early infancy and the task of loving, protecting and self-regulating that faces their parents. We finish the book with some concluding thoughts in Chapter 10.

We should provide a few comments about the terms used in this book. To begin with "the baby" – we are here referring to preverbal babies, indeed this is one of the key points that differentiates the PPIP model from interventions that address zero- to three-year-olds or zero- to five-year-olds. When it comes to parents, we use the word "parent" here to refer to that person who is a love-object and provider of attachment experiences to the baby, it may be a father or a mother, a grandparent or a foster-parent. We chose the term parent rather than caregiver to emphasize the intimacy of this relationship.

References

Alvarez, A. (2010). Levels of analytic work and levels of pathology: The work of calibration. *International Journal of PsychoAnalysis, 91*(4), 859–878. Doi:10.1111/j.1745-8315.2010.00284.x

The Association for Infant Mental Health UK. (2019). *Infant mental health competencies framework: Pregnancy to 2 years.* https://aimh.uk/infant-mental-health-competencies-framework/.

Baradon, T. (2013). *New beginnings manual: Community.* Ana Freud Centre. Unpublished manual.

Baradon, T., Sleed, M., Atkins, R., Campbell, C., Fagin, A., Van Schaick, R., & Fonagy, P. (2017). New beginnings: A time-limited, group intervention for high-risk infants and mothers. In H. Steele & M. Steele (Eds.), *Handbook of attachment-based interventions.* New York, NY: Guilford Press.

Beebe, B., Jaffe, J., Lachman, F., Feldstein, S., Crown, C., & Jasnow, M. (2000). Systems models in development and psychoanalysis: The case of vocal rhythm, coordination and attachment. *Infant Mental Health Journal, 21*(1–2), 99–122.

Beebe, B., & Steele, M. (2013). How does microanalysis of mother-infant communication inform maternal sensitivity and infant attachment? *Attachment & Human Development, 15*(5–6), 583–602. Doi:10.1080/14616734.2013.841050

Byrne, G., Sleed, M., Midgley, N., Fearon, P., Mein, C., Bateman, A., & Fonagy, P. (2019). Lighthouse Parenting Programme: Description and pilot evaluation of mentalization-based treatment to address child maltreatment. *Clinical Child Psychology and Psychiatry, 24*(4), 680–693. Doi:10.1177/1359104518807741

Ensink, K., Begin, M., Normandin, L., & Fonagy, P. (2017). Parental reflective functioning as a moderator of child internalizing difficulties in the context of child sexual abuse. *Psychiatry Research, 257*, 361–366. Doi:10.1016/j.psychres.2017.07.051

Fonagy, P., & Bateman, A. W. (2006). Mechanisms of change in mentalization-based treatment of BPD. *Journal of Clinical Psychology, 62*(4), 411–430. Doi:10.1002/jclp.20241

Fonagy, P., Moran, G. S., Edgcumbe, R., Kennedy, H., & Target, M. (1993). The roles of mental representations and mental processes in therapeutic action. *Psychoanalytic Study of the Child, 48*, 9–48. Doi:10.1080/00797308.1993.11822377

Fonagy, P., Steele, H., & Steele, M. (1991). Maternal representations of attachment during pregnancy predict the organization of infant-mother attachment at one year of age. *Child Development, 62*(5), 891–905. Doi:10.1111/j.1467–8624.1991.tb01578.x

Fonagy, P., Steele, M., Moran, G., Steele, H., & Higgitt, A. (1993). Measuring the ghost in the nursery: An empirical study of the relation between parents' mental representations of childhood experiences and their infants' security of attachment. *Journal of the American Psychoanalytic Association, 41*(4), 957–989.

Hrdy, S. B. (2011). *Mothers and others.* Boston, MA: Harvard University Press.

Hurry, A. (1998). Psychoanalysis and developmental therapy. In A. Hurry (Ed.), *Psychoanalysis and developmental theory* (pp. 32–73). London: Karnac.

Keaveny, E., Midgley, N., Asen, E., Bevington, D., Fearon, P., Fonagy, P., . . . Wood, S. D. (2012). Minding the family mind: The development and initial evaluation of mentalization-based treatment for families. In N. Midgley & I. Vrouva (Eds.), *Minding the child* (pp. 98–112). Hove, UK: Routledge.

Luyten, P., Campbell, C., Allison, E., & Fonagy, P. (2020). The mentalizing approach to psychopathology: State of the art and future directions. *Annual Review of Clinical Psychology, 16*, 297–325. Doi:10.1146/annurev-clinpsy-071919–015355

Madigan, S., Bakermans-Kranenburg, M. J., Van Ijzendoorn, M. H., Moran, G., Pederson, D. R., & Benoit, D. (2006). Unresolved states of mind, anomalous parental behavior, and disorganized attachment: A review and meta-analysis of a transmission gap. *Attachment and Human Development, 8*(2), 89–111. Doi:10.1080/14616730600774458

Malle, B. (2021). The tree of social cognition: Hierarchically organized capacities of mentalizing. In G. M. & O. K. N. (Eds.), *The neural basis of mentalizing* (pp. 337–370). Cham: Springer.

Midgley, N., & Vrouva, I. (Eds.). (2012). *Minding the child: Mentalization-based interventions with children, young people and their families.* London, UK: Routledge.

Sadler, L. S., Slade, A., Close, N., Webb, D. L., Simpson, T., Fennie, K., & Mayes, L. C. (2013). Minding the Baby: Enhancing reflectiveness to improve early health and relationship outcomes in an interdisciplinary home visiting program. *Infant Mental Health Journal, 34*(5), 391–405. Doi:10.1002/imhj.21406

Slade, A., Holland, M. L., Ordway, M. R., Carlson, E. A., Jeon, S., Close, N., . . . Sadler, L. S. (2019). Minding the Baby®: Enhancing parental reflective functioning and infant attachment in an attachment-based, interdisciplinary home visiting program. *Development and Psychopathology*. Doi:10.1017/S0954579418001463

Sleed, M., Baradon, T., & Fonagy, P. (2013). New beginnings for mothers and babies in prison: A cluster randomized controlled trial. *Attachment and Human Development*, *15*(4), 349–367. Doi:10.1080/14616734.2013.782651

Steele, H., Perez, A., Segal, F., & Steele, M. (2016). Maternal Adult Attachment Interview (AAI) collected during pregnancy predicts reflective functioning in AAIs from their first-born children 17 years later. *International Journal of Developmental Science*, *10*(3–4), 117–124. Doi:10.3233/dev-16201

Stern, D. N. (1985). *The interpersonal world of the infant: A view from psychoanalysis and developmental psychology*. New York, NY: Basic Books.

Stern, D. N. (1995). *The motherhood constellation: A unified view of parent-infant psychotherapy*. New York: Basic Books.

Suchman, N. E. (2016). Mothering from the Inside Out: A mentalization-based therapy for mothers in treatment for drug addiction. *International Journal of Birth and Parent Education*, *3*(4), 19–24.

Suchman, N. E., Berg, A., Abrahams, L., Abrahams, T., Adams, A., Cowley, B., . . . Voges, J. (2020). Mothering from the Inside Out: Adapting an evidence-based intervention for high-risk mothers in the Western Cape of South Africa. *Development and Psychopathology*, *32*(1), 105–122. Doi:10.1017/S0954579418001451

Suchman, N. E., DeCoste, C. L., McMahon, T. J., Dalton, R., Mayes, L. C., & Borelli, J. (2017). Mothering from the Inside Out: Results of a second randomized clinical trial testing a mentalization-based intervention for mothers in addiction treatment. *Development and Psychopathology*, *29*(2), 617–636. Doi:10.1017/S0954579417000220

Tronick, E., Als, H., Adamson, L., Wise, S., & Brazelton, T. B. (1978). The infant's response to entrapment between contradictory messages in face-to-face interaction. *Journal of the American Academy of Child and Adolescent Psychiatry*, *17*(1), 1–13.

Winnicott, D. W. (1953). Transitional objects and transitional phenomena: A study of the first not-me possession. *International Journal of Psycho-Analysis*, *34*(2), 89–97.

2 Theoretical framework

Parent-infant relationships

The idea that childhood experiences shape later development – "the Child is father of the Man" (William Wordsworth) – is a familiar concept. Research evidence on the role of nature and nurture is increasingly suggestive of processes that draw on an interaction between the two. Indeed, the unique temperamental presence of even very young babies is testament to the richness of innate and individual selfhood. However, we have strong biomedical and clinical research evidence that indicates the powerful ways in which the early environment can shape genetic potential in development as the patterns of early experiences become embedded in the brain, metabolic and immune systems. And on a real-life, clinical level, the environment of intimate relationships (relational environment), which is the developmental environment of the baby, is something that can potentially be changed in order to support infants, with their different natures and genetic propensities, as they encounter the world. The majority of parents, the "ordinary devoted" (Winnicott, 2016a) mothers and fathers, provide their babies with sufficiently predictable, safe and nurturing relational environments. Winnicott (1960, p. 588) suggests: "Human infants cannot start to be except under certain conditions. These conditions . . . are part of the psychology of the infant. Infants come into being differently according to whether the conditions are favourable or unfavourable". He further explains his view that "the . . . conditions do not determine the infant's potential. This is inherited . . . [but] it is accepted that the inherited potential of an infant cannot become an infant unless linked to maternal care" (Winnicott, 1960, p. 588). The maternal provision that Winnicott describes is based on the mother's identification with her infant, such that "she knows what the infant may be feeling like . . . minute to minute" (Winnicott, 2016b). Knowing her infant is the basis for her "holding and handling" that allows him or her to be sheltered from

DOI: 10.4324/9781003024323-2

external impingements that would disturb his true self-development. The British psychoanalyst Bion further described the process in which mother takes into her "maternal reverie" the raw experiences of the infant and transforms them into metabolized elements of experience that the baby can use to get to know himself (Bion, 1962). The feelings, experiences and sensations of the baby – which are incomprehensible, and potentially overwhelming to the baby – are "digested" by the mother by her making sense of them and giving meaning to those sensations for the baby. The infant whose physio-emotional states are consistently not "contained" (Bion, 1963) in his/her interactions with the parent can suffer devastating anxiety and is at risk of fragmentation in their sense of self. We should add, by way of a note, that Winnicott and Bion tended to write of the mother in relation to the infant, as the mother was generally assumed to take this role. But we now tend to use the term "parent" to denote how this care can be provided by either or both parents or other caregiver, to reflect a growing social awareness that this primary early role is taken on by whoever acts as the crucial intimate caring figure.

The attachment researcher Mary Ainsworth developed the ground-breaking concept of "maternal sensitivity" as a result of her naturalistic field research observing mothers and infants in their own settings. The concept of sensitivity remains a gold-standard gauge of parenting associ-ated with secure attachment in the baby (Verhage et al., 2016): infants whose parents are more sensitive are more likely, but by no means guar-anteed (Granqvist et al., 2017), to display secure attachment relationships. Sensitivity is predicated on the parent's ability to perceive and infer the meaning behind his or her infant's behaviour and to respond to them promptly and appropriately.

Mind-mindedness and mentalizing have contributed other ways of thinking about parental sensitivity. Mentalizing theory suggests that the infant's sense of self is scaffolded by the parent's capacity to imagine the infant's mental state and then, critically, to reflect the infant's experience back to them in what have been described as "marked mirroring" interactions. These interactions involve the adult accurately representing the child's experience in the moment in a regulated way and reflecting back to the child these representations of his/her child's state in a manageable, non-overwhelming way. (There are parallels here with Bion's concept of reverie and returning to the infant his previously inchoate experience in a way that the infant can take in and make use of.) There is now an extensive body of evidence that shows that a parent's capacity to mentalize their infant is associated with secure attachment and supporting the development of their child's ability to mentalize (Luyten, Campbell, Allison, & Fonagy, 2020).

In tandem with the research and clinical characterizations of parental contributions to healthy development, infant research in recent decades has reshaped our view of the baby – from passive recipient of parental care to an active partner who influences the parent-infant relationship. We now know that infants are born with cross-modal perceptual abilities that provide for seeking out, perceiving and interacting with others who position themselves as social partners. Through the perception of correspondences – "you are like me" and "I am like you" – both infant and partner (and we here focus on the parents as infants' conversational partners) are able to apprehend the inner feeling state of the other and whether the state is shared (Meltzoff & Moore, 1998; Stern, 1985; Trevarthen & Aitken, 2001). Developmental research into intersubjectivity – the sharing of subjective states by two or more individuals – has shown that emotional coordination is formed by reciprocal "micro-momentary shifts over time" (Beebe & Lachmann, 2014, p. 28) as each partner anticipates the behavioural flow of self and other. Moreover, infants have the capacity to detect pattern and order in events occurring over time (Saffran & Kirkham, 2018). With repeated experience they create procedural expectations regarding the sequence of their own actions and in relation to those of the partner, with accompanying arousal patterns (Beebe et al., 2010; Beebe & Lachmann, 2014; Stern, 1985). What is characteristic of these intersubjective studies is that although parents and babies tend to bring to their relationship predispositions – the infant's make-up and temperament and the parent's experiences, representations, make-up and temperament – we also see in-the-moment dynamic co-construction of relating. The Boston Change Process Study Group have used the term "implicit relational knowing" – the procedural knowledge of both parent and infant about how to "do relationships" with others (Lyons-Ruth, 1998, 1999; Stern, 1998). The interactions that form this embodied relational knowing mostly occur much too quickly to be registered consciously. Daniel Stern evocatively used William Blake's idea of "a world in a grain of sand" to convey how small, micro-interactions contain and build the stuff of relational experience out of which human development is built (Stern, 2010). It is important to note that there is also significant cultural input into ways of being with the other, including sharing emotional states, which feed into the implicit relational knowing, those cultural expectations about ways of behaving that constitute part of this procedural knowledge (Feldman, 2007). A recent international review of mentalizing, for example, has found that the way in which we perceive the mental states of others varies in different cultures, with a notable difference between collectivistic cultures and individualistic cultures. In collectivistic cultures, which emphasize the needs and goals of the group as a whole over the needs and desires of each individual, there is a greater tendency to mentalize others. By contrast, in individualistic cultures, the mentalizing profile tends to be more focused on the self (Aival-Naveh, Rothschild-Yakar, & Kurman, 2019).

Of course, no matter how good we are at reading mental states, interactions are not matched and synchronous all the time, and parenting should not be expected to be "perfect". We return to Winnicott's idea of "good enough" mothers (now an idea applied to both parents): that parents try their best to put the needs of their child ahead of their own but also inevitably fail them. Furthermore, babies and children actually benefit when their mothers fail them in manageable ways, that is, in ways that do not overwhelm the baby (e.g., taking just a little bit too long to present the food or pick him/her up from the cot after a nap). "Good enough" is an important concept linking parental behaviour and infant security of attachment to that parent. Beebe and colleagues' research shows that a mid-range model of interactive contingency (i.e., modifying behaviour and coordinating it with the partner) is associated with security of attachment in the baby, while both high (hyper-vigilant, intrusive) and low (withdrawn) levels of interactive contingency predict insecure attachment (Beebe et al., 2008). Tronick's research found that 70% of the time, mothers and their 6-month-old babies were not in synchrony; thus, normal infants experience a large number of mismatches in their ordinary, daily interactions with their parents. Mismatches generate negative affect, but when the miscommunications are repaired – termed "interactive repair" – both baby and parent experience positive affect which replaces the negative, and the baby may begin to learn that such experiences are the stuff of life rather than catastrophes (Tronick, 1989). Interactive repair, Tronick suggests, contributes to security of attachment (Gianino & Tronick, 1988). Hopkins, an early parent-infant psychotherapist in the UK, describes the possible negative outcomes for the baby of "too-good" parenting. She proposes that when mothering is too well adapted to infant needs, the infant is deprived of agency and "of possibilities for negotiation, concern and reparation" (Hopkins, 1996, p. 47) and their trajectory of development is negatively impacted. Mentalizing theory has also placed a strong emphasis on how inaccuracies and uncertainty about mental states are a fact of life: by their very nature, thoughts and feelings are not visible, clearly delineated or knowable with total conviction. Indeed, we often make errors in our assumptions about what our own motivations are. Mentalization-based treatment suggests that we cannot be entirely certain and correct in what we assume about mental states, and that rigid certainty is a marker of poor mentalizing (Bateman & Fonagy, 2016). Rather, the approach assumes that being able to tolerate the fact that we all make mistakes in mentalizing and that we need to be curious and open to being corrected and making adjustments in what we assume about mental states is essential to adaptive social functioning. In terms of caring for an infant, we need to accept the fact that we will all at moments misread our baby – the real issue is, are we prepared to be "corrected" by our baby and be open to adjusting our behaviour accordingly. An infant who finds their corrective communications about their needs responded to is, in mentalizing terms, being treated as in possession of a separate agentive mind, which their parent is interested and invested in – such exchanges show to the infant that mental states matter.

An observation illustrates how all these theories, ideas and concepts are enacted in small, everyday moments of interaction:

> Emory (8 months) woke up and turned his head in the direction of his mother, smiling. She was sitting across the room talking to a friend and did not notice his awakening. Emory babbled quietly to himself. Hearing his voice, his mother looked over at him and softly said "Hello Emory, you not sleeping anymore?" He smiled again at his mother but then noticed the friend and his eyes appeared to widen and his smile dropped. He quickly looked back to his mother, *who had already started to get up and was moving over to him.* She was saying softly "Hello baby . . . who is this here . . .?" Emory had stretched out his arms towards his approaching mother and as he was beginning to cry out, she arrived in front of him. She talked gently as she bent down towards him, saying "Hello, sleepy . . . our friend has come to see us . . . *did you get a fright? . . . you remember . . .".* Emory reached his arms up towards his mother, beaming. They held eye contact with each other. She was also smiling.

Emory wakes up and, hearing his mother's voice, turns with an expectation of a positive exchange – in anticipation of which he smiles at her. However, mother is busy and does not notice his wakened state. Emory holds on to a feeling of safety from his mother's audible proximity, and plays by himself. However, inevitably, stressors occur in the life of a baby even with good enough parenting. In Emory's case, the visitor was unexpected and he got a fright when he saw her. We may think that his mother intuitively (through identification or resonance with the baby's state) drew his fright into her maternal reverie, made meaning of it (mentalizing) and returned his experience to him in words that were scaffolded by matching gentle, caressing tone, facial expression (marked mirroring): "*Did you get a fright? . . . you remember?*" Thus, Emory's mother provided ordinary hold-ing and handling that pre-empted catastrophic anxieties and extreme dis-tress. Using a framework of maternal sensitivity, we see that Emory's stress was reduced by his mother's quick perception of his distress, understand-ing of its cause and behavioural response to reassure. Research suggests that sensitivity to distress or in distressing contexts is a significant predictor of attachment security over and above sensitivity to non-distress cues or in a non-distressing context (Del Carmen, Pedersen, Huffman, & Bryan, 1993). Indeed, stresses that the parents buffer, as Emory's mother did, actu-ally contribute to the development of healthy stress response systems in the child, as opposed to stressors that are not mediated by the parents, which become overwhelming and can cumulatively create "toxic stress" for the baby (Center on the Developing Child, 2015).

When Emory's little crisis occurs – that is, when the expectation of seeing mother is contaminated by threat (the unexpected presence of the visitor), there was a finely-timed dance between his call for help and her arrival at his cot to comfort him – his mother *had already started to get up and was moving over to him*. A sense of safety is restored through eye con-tact, outreaching arms and smiles.

Emory and his mother also demonstrate how it is through ordinary caretaking – the parents' way of holding him, talking to him, their habitual bodily handling – that the baby gets to know his parents and himself. Through caretaking ministrations, micro-interactions that occur so quickly that they are not available to the conscious recall but which are registered procedurally – that is, at an embodied level – the infant forms representations of what the world is like. If the experiences reinforce the expectancies over time, they will form the basis for the infant's repre-sentational world and internal working models – a template for future relationships based on early attachment experiences (Bretherton & Mun-holland, 2008).

Consider, for example, the differences in the experience of babies Amos and John, both aged three months. Amos has been lying on his tummy for a few minutes and is beginning to fret. His father crouches down and brings his face close to his son's his face and asks "What's up? Are you getting sick of facing the blanket? Come on." The father tucks his hand under Amos and says, "I'm going to give you a break". Amos is lifted gently and placed against his father's chest. His head rests against his father's heartbeat and almost immediately his eyes begin to close. John has also been lying on his tummy for a few minutes and is beginning to fret. His father approaches him from behind and lifts him. John looks startled and his body stiffens. Father turns him to place him against his (father's) chest. John is rigid, with wide open eyes. Father strokes his back until John starts to relax and falls asleep.

We imagine that John's experience is split between fright (being suddenly lifted from the solid holding of the mat, to feel that he was floundering in the open air) on the one hand and comfort (father's chest and heartbeat) on the other. This experience may have been confusing for him since his father was both the source of the shock and the succour. At the same time, John's startled response and rigidity may have created for the father a sense that he was struggling against a difficult or rejecting baby. As a one-off event, Father's quick soothing of John after his startle illustrates paternal sensitivity and John's equilibrium is easily restored. However, if this manner of interaction were to continue, a broad-sweeping hypothesis about John's developmental trajectory of attachment representations could be that the representation he may gradually build is mixed, holding procedural memories of both startle and comfort with father. Amos, by contrast, has a smooth experience of his father's attention being directed towards him in an enquiring and reassuring way that prepares Amos for being lifted, and he experiences his father's care and attention with no attendant tension. He is likely to develop a more straightforward representation of father as a predictable and reliably safe attachment figure. Baby Amos's father in turn finds himself quickly rewarded by his baby's response, introducing a mutual expectation of smoothness of interaction with the other.

So, what might be the capacities parents draw on to provide growth-promoting environments? A go-to explanation is based on a transgenerational model of parenting: "if you were well enough parented yourself, it's probably all fairly easy: you have memories inside yourself, conscious and unconscious, to draw on" (Daws & de Rementeria, 2015, p. 52). A fundamental thesis in psychoanalysis is that good experiences form the basis for identifications with good caretaking objects which will populate the individual's inner world with positive attachment representations. To an extent, the proposition of transgenerational parenting is borne out in attachment-informed studies, such as the classic "Measuring the ghost in the nursery" study (Fonagy, Steele, Moran, Steele, & Higgitt, 1993), which established high concordance between attachment representations of the parent with attachment status of their child; sensitive and responsive patterns of maternal behaviour were observed more frequently in women classified as securely attached (and conversely). The authors' search for an explanatory pathway led them to make links between maternal sensitivity and the capacity for mentalizing. They concluded that

> cross-generational prediction of security is possible in part because attachment security in infancy is based on parental sensitivity to, and understanding of, the infant's mental world. The parent's capacity

to generate a psychological world for the infant is dependent on coherent representations of the mental world of self and other. . . . The coherence of the parents' perception of their past derives from an unhindered capacity to observe and reflect upon their own mental functioning . . . This coherence forms the bridge of attachment security between the generations. It is the precondition for the parent's ability to provide an "expectable" or "good-enough" mental environment for the infant.

(Fonagy et al., 1993, p. 987)

We suggest that coherent internal narratives emerge from truthful and inclusive dialogue with the other:

"Coherent", or "open", dialogue is characterised . . . by parental "openness" to the state of mind of the child, including the entire array of the child's communications, so that particular affective or motive states of the child (anger, passion, distress) are not foreclosed from intersubjective sharing and regulation.

(Lyons-Ruth, 1999, p. 583)

In our view, the ability to accept the full range of emotions, negative as well as positive, is particularly important in managing normal ambivalence towards one's baby. Ambivalence – loving and hostile feelings, wishes for closeness and for distance, compassion and coldness, are seen as characteristic of ordinary relationships. Mostly these feelings are fluid and the intensity comes and goes. Thus, Daws and de Rementaria caution parents:

You will not escape having mixed, even hostile feelings towards your baby but you will be able to keep them in perspective and not let that interfere with caring for and loving your baby . . . just as your parents responded to you.

(Daws & de Rementaria, 2015, pp. 52–53)

In suggesting that a good enough mother (parent) will keep her negative moments in perspective and not let them interfere with caring for her baby, these authors show the way for the next generation to experience and then model holding the range of feeling, without enactment.

Yet it is not only past experiences that may offer sources of resilience for ordinary good enough parenting. Current attachment figures are of pivotal importance, as are the quality of the couple relationship, extended family, availability of social support – including, at times, the professional network – associated with adult perinatal functioning and parenting (Angley, Divney, Magriples, & Kershaw, 2015; Leahy-Warren, McCarthy, & Corcoran, 2012). We also know that childhood adversity can trigger negative transferences (transference is a psychoanalytic term used to describe circumstances when feelings about a significant figure, often the individual's early attachment figure, are directed towards a different person in the present). The transfer of negative feelings and expectations can result in "social thinning" (Goemans, Viding, & McCrory, 2021) of present supportive relationships and, thereby potentially, isolation and mental health difficulties.

Fathers and paternal function

With the birth of a child a triad is formed – whether or not both parents are present in the daily life of the infant. When one of the parents is absent, the child will learn about that parent through the image and feelings about him or her that are invariably conveyed by the parent who is present. The child is "introduced" thereby to his or her (absent) parent in the caregiving-parent's mind, often without the opportunity for verifying, modifying or dismissing that representation through real-life experience. In this way, every child has an internal father-person.

The classic psychoanalytic position tasks the father who is present in the life of his infant with facilitating the separation of the baby from his or her mother – the separating third – thus rescuing the child from engulfment with mother, supporting individuation and opening the child to the world (Abelin, 1976; Lacan, 1977; Mahler & Gosliner, 1955; Paquette, 2004; von Klitzing & Stadelmann, 2011). These gendered paternal functions are seen to facilitate the development of the infant along a trajectory from dyadic to triadic-Oedipal to familial and group relating.

There is a certain cultural bias in this classical view of the father. The first assumes the baby is socialized into a dyad, whereas in some cultures the socialization is into the group which emphasizes "person-oriented sensitivities as dependence, empathy, indulgence, accommodation, compliance, and propriety in interpersonal relationships" as opposed to individualism (Bornstein, Cote, Haynes, Suwalsky, & Bakeman, 2012). Furthermore, in a context of changing ideas about gender and family constructions, there is growing exploration of "paternal function" in the life of the baby as distinct from the contribution of a male father's active presence. For example, Davies and Eagle suggest that the third person/object who allows for triadic relating can be anyone who fulfils functions such as helping separate the baby from a fused relationship with mother or primary parent, and supporting affect regulation, particularly the management of aggression (Davies & Eagle, 2013). This approach of distinguishing between "functions" and "functionary" widens the lens to include alternate family structures, so that the "third" person in the triad may traverse gender or generational binaries, or even physical presence (Golombok, 2017).

However, while expanding the lens of triangulation to reflect different family structures, there are still many families where the father is present and active in the life of the infant. Here, too, there has been a cultural shift in western societies from a view of the father as the enforcer of discipline, boundary setting, and regulator of infant aggression to a view of the father as nurturant and closely involved in all aspects of his baby's care. Indeed, research suggests that increased caregiving activity helps stimulate the construction of the neural circuits that underpin nurturing behaviours in fathers (Abraham et al., 2014). Furthermore, there is a greater tendency to view a combination of maternal and paternal functions as embodied in parents of either gender.

While there may be increasing areas of overlap, it has also been argued that fathers bring unique dimensions to their baby's experience and development and these increase the infant's resilience and exploration. Feldman's research found that levels of arousal in the infants during mother-infant interactions moved between low and medium levels and high positive affect surfaced gradually in a social episode (Feldman, 2003). By contrast, during father-infant play, positive arousal was high, sudden and organized in multiple peaks. These peaks appeared more frequently as play progressed. Research has also indicated that fathers can introduce behaviours that would be experienced as frightening were they to come from the mother, as long as the father was also able to notice and de-escalate arousal and reassure his baby if the features of the play became overwhelming (Hazen, 2010).

There are cultural and economic influences on how fathers' and mothers' roles are shaped and the access fathers have to their young infants. However, the father's readiness and ability to interact with their baby may be curbed by intrapsychic conflicts over assuming their role as father (Emanuel, 2002; Trowell, 2002), or by difficulties for the baby's mother in "letting him in" (Marks, 2002). The mother can critically influence the father's relationship with his baby. Studies show that marital satisfaction and spousal support are closely linked to fathering and father-child relationships (Gordon & Feldman, 2008). A supportive mother facilitates closer father-child relationships, or alternatively a mother may gatekeep their relationship, puncturing the bond because of her own conflicts or because of real-life concerns about the father's parenting. Situations may then be developed in which

> a father who is physically present might nevertheless be lived as symbolically lost, absent or dead in the child's inner world depending once again on the father's own personality and *on the way the mother invests and speaks of him to the child.*
>
> (McDougall, 1989, p. 239, italics added)

Consideration of these issues – father's own conflicts in assuming full fatherhood and how the mother supports or hinders the father-infant relationship, as well as spousal issues that spill into parenting of the infant – are all arguments in favour of including fathers (or father figures) in the therapy whenever possible. As Cowan and Cowan propose "fathering is a family affair" (Cowan, Cowan, Heming, & Miller, 1991).

The capacity for triangulation

As Fonagy and Target note, "the physical presence [of the father] may be neither sufficient nor necessary for triangulation to evolve" (Target & Fonagy, 2002, p. 57). In light of the previous discussion, we may expand "father" to encompass any significant attachment figures who may potentially be a "third". Whether or not a parent can allow their infant a full and rounded relationship with another will depend on each parent's capacities for triangulation (Baradon, 2019). This refers to the internal capacity to enter a psychic triangular space wherein relationships with and between significant others can exist; for example, between mother-baby, father-baby and mother-father within the overall system of the family. As discussed earlier, in differing family constellations it may be father, same-sex parent, grandparent or any other person who is a love-object and provider of attachment experiences to the baby. The capacity for triangulation entails, as described by Britton, tolerating "the possibility of being a participant in a relationship and observed by a third person as well as being an observer of a relationship between two people" (Britton, 2004, p. 47). Research shows that infants of 3–4 months can already share their attention with both parents if supported in this (Fivaz-Depcursinge & Corboz-Warnery, 1999; von Klitzing, Simoni, Amsler, & Bürgin, 1999). Parental support for their baby's interest in, and bids for, the other parent depends on whether the position of the third is tenable for each adult. For example, the demands of triadification may reach into conflicts of the past such as early feelings of envy and exclusion in their family of origin; triggering such feelings might negatively impact the new family's interactions.

The capacity for triangulation has a central influence on whether or not the parents come together to co-parent their infant within a collaborative structure. It can be satisfying in the context of shared aspirations for the child and pleasure within the triad, but it can also be a complex stance to hold. For example, von Klitzing and colleagues demonstrated that triadic interaction in play could easily be disturbed by latent parental partnership conflicts (von Klitzing et al., 1999). In well-functioning triadic constellations

> experiencing differences between the mother and the father object, between their interactional styles and their ways of dealing with the child's needs, enables the child not only to experience him/herself in the mirror of the object, but also to find him/herself in relationship with differing objects.
>
> (von Klitzing, 2019, p. 23)

The wider network

Child development is relational not only in the sense of the dyadic, triadic and familial contexts but also within the wider context of influential relationships. Working with the parents of young children in some ways throws into even starker relief the importance of social support and cultural ecology around a family. Being in the position of caring for a young infant calls on a parent's physical and emotional resources in an almost uniquely intensive way that means that additional support and scaffolding for the parent can be of critical importance to both parent's and infant's wellbeing. Positive social support of family, friends and organizational networks ("social capital") contributes to wellbeing, attitudes and behaviours during pregnancy and transitioning to parenthood (Angley et al., 2015; Leahy-Warren et al., 2012). Greater maternal social support is related to more secure infant attachment (Crockenberg, 1981) through maternal wellbeing and the enhancement of reciprocity and mutual gratification within the relationship. Interviews with parents of infants and small children have emphasized the value they placed on social support in the here and now:

> Although they varied in the amount wished for, all parents expressed a need to share experiences with others, without being judged, problematised or instrumentalised. Those not yet experiencing it wished also to feel connected to their living environment in some ways.
>
> (Geens, 2015)

Many of the parents who are struggling in the perinatal period describe social isolation. While this may be due to external factors such as a move or migration, we are also increasingly aware of the phenomenon of social thinning (Goemans et al., 2021). By this is meant that old expectations of rejection drive withdrawal or lashing out such that the other withdraws. For some isolated parent/parents, the PPIP model may provide an initial experience of feeling that there is an interested world around their baby; it seeks to use this validating experience to create a sense of the infant being seen and appreciated, the work of parenting acknowledged, its difficulties recognized and its satisfactions celebrated. Moreover, PPIP has always been concerned with being accessible and reaching those who need help most (see Chapter 4). It also actively supports the joining up with the wider network of support around a family (described more fully in Chapters 4 and 8).

Mentalizing theory too has placed increasing emphasis on the social environment around the child in supporting their development: while immediate attachment relationships are still understood as the incubator of mentalizing in infancy, there is an increasing emphasis on the role of wider mentalizing or non-mentalizing social systems in supporting this process (Fonagy et al., 2021; Fonagy, Luyten, Allison, & Campbell, 2017a, 2017b). In relation to infancy, we would argue that the experience of a parent who is functioning in a relentlessly non-mentalizing social system, whether that is on a domestic, institutional or community level, in which their agency, sense of self and capacity for affect regulation is not recognized or supported may face a greater struggle to hold onto their own capacity to mentalize; this would include mentalizing their baby. This is because (as we will describe in more detail in Chapter 5), mentalizing is fundamentally interactive: not only does the capacity to mentalize initially develop in the context of interactions with others, it also continues to remain influenced by the mentalizing capacity of those others. We may also hypothesize the non-mentalizing environment, titrated to the baby through the parent's reflective difficulties, would impact the baby's − embodied attempts to seek a mentalizing other.

Culture

The PPIP model regards infants as intrinsically part of their culture: "There is not a child and a culture, but always a child in culture" (Richter, 2010, p. 533). Bornstein suggests that meaning-making mediates the "differences in environments, emotions and interactions (which) characterize how different cultures shape human development" (Bornstein, 2010, p. 36). For example, Dimitrova discusses maternal communications about the infant's cultural world (e.g., about the safety of the object, how it can/ should be used in triadic mother-infant-object interactions) (Dimitrova,

2010). She suggests that most of the time parents are not aware of the fact that they transmit such conventional knowledge because it is embedded in their own cultural procedural knowledge but, developmentally for the child, it is through these triadic interactions that this joint engagement and attention consolidates and early communication develops. Thus, the field of infant mental health, in its ever-wider cultural milieux, has become more attentive to the richness and value of the social depth that comes from supporting an infant not just in their dyad, or even triadic and familial context, but in their cultural world too.

An ecological perspective

An ecological approach posits that while the immediate microsystem of the family is the most significant for babies and young children, to understand a child's development we must look not only at the child and his or her immediate environment, but also at the interaction of the larger environment of communities, cultural values, laws and organizations. In the ecological-contextual view, parent and child are at the centre of inter-linked nested systems (Bronfenbrenner, 1986), each of which outlines an environmental context to the interactions that take place between parents and infant.

There is tension between psychological interventions that aim to heighten self-other reflectivity and the situation of families who are enduring experiences such as poverty, discrimination, inadequate local services and institutional/legal injustice. Extensive evidence demonstrates that such environmental risk factors impact mental health and children's developmental prospects (Liu, Mustanski, Dick, Bolland, & Kertes, 2017; Lund et al., 2018). It is sometimes argued that the port of entry to the wellbeing of the infant is via change in the structural socio-economic conditions surrounding families and communities (Burns, 2015) rather than therapeutic programs which may pathologize the family. We acknowledge that view and have considerable sympathy for the need for action at those levels, and believe we need to be aware of the potential insensitivity of discounting the real experiences and difficulties of parents in some circumstances. On the other hand, this book is about relating to the minds of parents and infants in the most personal intimate way and making space for psychological processing of their idiomatic experience. There is some evidence for the importance and efficacy of this for the wellbeing of parent and infant, even in very dire situations (Cooper et al., 2009).

In some intervention programmes, awareness of the impact of deprivation has resulted in extending the role of the therapist (Lieberman & Van Horn, 2008). In PPIP, socio-economic and power hardships are particularly attended to in the clinical work in relation to the impact they have on parental functioning, inasmuch as the mental health vulnerabilities, stressors and instability that can be associated with exposure to social-economic risk factors can impinge on a parent's capacity to engage with their infant. Problems in the situation of a family vis a vis systems surrounding them, such as poverty or discrimination, are addressed through activating a network of providers around the child and family.

References

Abelin, E. L. (1976). Some further observations and comments on the earliest role of the father. *International Journal of Psycho-Analysis, 56*, 293–301.

Abraham, E., Hendler, T., Shapira-Lichter, I., Kanat-Maymon, Y., Zagoory-Sharon, O., & Feldman, R. (2014). Father's brain is sensitive to childcare experiences. *Proceedings of the National Academy of Sciences USA, 111*(27), 9792–9797. doi:10.1073/pnas.1402569111

Aival-Naveh, E., Rothschild-Yakar, L., & Kurman, J. (2019). Keeping culture in mind: A systematic review and initial conceptualization of mentalizing from a cross-cultural perspective. *Clinical Psychology: Science and Practice, 26*(4). doi:10.1111/cpsp.12300

Angley, M., Divney, A., Magriples, U., & Kershaw, T. (2015). Social support, family functioning and parenting competence in adolescent parents. *Maternal and Child Health Journal, 19*(1), 67–73. doi:10.1007/s10995–014–1496-x

Baradon, T. (2019). Working with the triad. In *Working with fathers in psychoanalytic parent-infant psychotherapy*. London: Routledge.

Bateman, A., & Fonagy, P. (2016). *Mentalization-based treatment for personality disorders: A practical guide*. Oxford, UK: Oxford University Press.

Beebe, B., Jaffe, J., Buck, K., Chen, H., Cohen, P., Feldstein, S., & Andrews, H. (2008). Six-week postpartum maternal depressive symptoms and 4-month mother-infant self- and interactive contingency. *Infant Mental Health Journal, 29*(5), 442–471. doi:10.1002/imhj.20191

Beebe, B., Jaffe, J., Markese, S., Buck, K., Chen, H., Cohen, P., . . . Feldstein, S. (2010). The origins of 12-month attachment: A microanalysis of 4-month mother-infant interaction. *Attachment and Human Development, 12*(1–2), 3–141. doi:10.1080/14616730903338985

Beebe, B., & Lachmann, F. M. (2014). *The origins of attachment: Infant research and adult treatment*. New York, NY: Routledge.

Bion, W. R. (1962). *Learning from experience*. London, UK: Heinemann.

Bion, W. R. (1963). *Elements of psycho-analysis*. London, UK: Heinemann.

Bornstein, M. H. (2010). From measurement to meaning in caregiving and culture: Current challenges and future perspectives. In C. Worthman, P. M. Plotsky, D. S. Schechter, & C. A. Cummings (Eds.), *Formative experiences: The interactions of caregiving, culture and developmental psychbiology* (pp. 36–50). Cambridge: Cambridge University Press.

Bornstein, M. H., Cote, L. R., Haynes, O. M., Suwalsky, J. T., & Bakeman, R. (2012). Modalities of infant-mother interaction in Japanese, Japanese American immigrant, and European American dyads. *Child Development*, *83*(6), 2073–2088. doi:10.1111/j.1467–8624.2012.01822.x

Bretherton, K., & Munholland, K. A. (2008). Internal working models in attachment relationships: Elaborating a central construct in attachment theory. In J. Cassidy & P. R. Shaver (Eds.), *Handbook of attachment: Theory, research and clinical applications* (2nd ed., pp. 102–127). New York, NY: Guilford Press.

Britton, R. (2004). Subjectivity, objectivity, and triangular space. *The Psychoanalytic Quarterly*, *73*(1), 47–62.

Bronfenbrenner, U. (1986). Ecology of the family as a context for human development: Research perspectives. *Developmental Psychology*, *22*(6), 723–742. doi:10. 1037//0012–1649.22.6.723

Burns, J. K. (2015). Poverty, inequality and a political economy of mental health. *Epidemiology and Psychiatric Sciences*, *24*(2), 107–113. doi:10.1017/S2045796015000086

Center on the Developing Child. (2015). *From best practices to breakthrough impacts: A science-based approach to building a more promising future for young children and families.* Cambridge, MA: Harvard Center on the Developing Child.

Cooper, P. J., Tomlinson, M., Swartz, L., Landman, M., Molteno, C., Stein, A., . . . Murray, L. (2009). Improving quality of mother-infant relationship and infant attachment in socioeconomically deprived community in South Africa: Randomised controlled trial. *BMJ*, *338*, b974. doi:10.1136/bmj.b974

Cowan, C. P., Cowan, P. A., Heming, G., & Miller, N. B. (1991). Becoming a family: Marriage, parenting, and child development. In P. A. Cowan & E. M. Hetherington (Eds.), *Family transitions* (pp. 79–109). Hillsdale: Lawrence Erlbaum Associates.

Crockenberg, S. B. (1981). Infant irritability, mother responsiveness, and social support influences on the security of infant-mother attachment. *Child Development*, *52*(3), 857–865.

Davies, N., & Eagle, G. (2013). Conceptualizing the paternal function: Maleness, masculinity, or thirdness? *Contemporary Psychoanalysis*, *49*(4), 559–585. doi:10.108 0/00107530.2013.10779264

Daws, D., & de Rementaria, A. (2015). *Finding your way with your baby: The emotional life of parents and babies.* Abingdon: Routledge.

Del Carmen, R., Pedersen, F., Huffman, L., & Bryan, Y. (1993). Dyadic distress management predicts security of attachment. *Infant Behavior and Development*, *16*, 131–147.

Dimitrova, N. (2010). Culture in infancy: An account of a way the object "sculpts" early development. *Psychology and Society*, *3*(1).

Emanuel, R. (2002). On becoming a father: Reflections from infant observation. In J. Trowell (Ed.), *The importance of fathers: A psychoanalytic re-evaluation* (pp. 131–146). Hove: Brunner-Routledge.

Feldman, R. (2003). Infant-mother and infant-father synchrony: The coregulation of positive arousal. *Infant Mental Health 24*, 1–23. doi:10.1002/imhj.10041

Feldman, R. (2007). Parent-infant synchrony and the construction of shared timing; physiological precursors, developmental outcomes, and risk conditions. *Journal of Child Psychology and Psychiatry*, *48*(3–4), 329–354. doi:10.1111/j.1469–7610.2006.01701.x

Fivaz-Depeursinge, E., & Corboz-Warnery, A. (1999). *The primary triangle: A developmental systems view of mothers, fathers, and infants.* New York: Basic Books.

Fonagy, P., Campbell, C., Constantinou, M., Higgitt, A., Allison, E., & Luyten, P. (2021). Culture and psychopathology. *Development and Psychopathology*, 1–16. doi:10.1017/S0954579421000092

Fonagy, P., Luyten, P., Allison, E., & Campbell, C. (2017a). What we have changed our minds about: Part 1: Borderline personality disorder as a limitation of resilience. *Borderline Personality Disorder and Emotion Dysregulation*, 4, 11. doi:10.1186/s40479-017-0061-9

Fonagy, P., Luyten, P., Allison, E., & Campbell, C. (2017b). What we have changed our minds about: Part 2: Borderline personality disorder, epistemic trust and the developmental significance of social communication. *Borderline Personality Disorder and Emotion Dysregulation*, 4, 9. doi:10.1186/s40479-017-0062-8

Fonagy, P., Steele, M., Moran, G., Steele, H., & Higgitt, A. (1993). Measuring the ghost in the nursery: An empirical study of the relation between parents' mental representations of childhood experiences and their infants' security of attachment. *Journal of the American Psychoanalytic Association*, 41(4), 957–989.

Geens, N. (2015). *Social support and social cohesion in services for young children: A study of interactions among parents and between parents and professionals.* (PhD). Ghent: Ghent University.

Gianino, A. F., & Tronick, E. Z. (1988). The mutual regulation model: The infant's self and interactive regulation and coping and defensive capacities. In T. M. Field, P. M. McCabe, & N. Schneiderman (Eds.), *Stress and coping across development* (pp. 47–68). Hillsdale, NJ: Lawrence Erlbaum Associates.

Goemans, A., Viding, E., & McCrory, E. (2021). Child maltreatment, peer victimization, and mental health: Neurocognitive perspectives on the cycle of victimization. *Trauma Violence Abuse*, 15248380211036393. doi:10.1177/15248380211036393

Golombok, S. (2017). Parenting in new family forms. *Current Opinion in Psychology*, 15, 76–80. doi:10.1016/j.copsyc.2017.02.004

Gordon, I., & Feldman, R. (2008). Synchrony in the triad: A microlevel process model of coparenting and parent-child interactions. *Family Process*, 47(4), 465–479. doi:10.1111/j.1545-5300.2008.00266.

Granqvist, P., Sroufe, L. A., Dozier, M., Hesse, E., Steele, M., van Ijzendoorn, M., . . . Duschinsky, R. (2017). Disorganized attachment in infancy: A review of the phenomenon and its implications for clinicians and policy-makers. *Attachment and Human Development*, 19(6), 534–558. doi:10.1080/14616734.2017.1354040

Hazen, N., McFarland, L., Jacobvitz, D., & Boyd-Soisson, E. (2010). Fathers' frightening and sensitive infant caregiving: Relations with fathers' attachment representations, father-infant attachment, and children's later development of emotion regulation and attention problems. *Early Development and Care*, 180, 51–69. doi:10.1080/03004430903414703

Hopkins, J. (1996). The dangers and deprivations of too-good mothering. *Journal of Child Psychotherapy*, 22(3), 407–422. doi:10.1080/00754179608254516

Lacan, J. (1977). *Écrits: A selection* (A. Sheridan, Trans.). London: Tavistock.

Leahy-Warren, P., McCarthy, G., & Corcoran, P. (2012). First-time mothers: Social support, maternal parental self-efficacy and postnatal depression. *Journal of Clinical Nursing*, 21(3–4), 388–397. doi:10.1111/j.1365-2702.2011.03701.x

Lieberman, A. F., & Van Horn, P. (2008). *Psychotherapy with infants and young children: Repairing the effects of stress and trauma on early attachment.* New York: Guilford Press.

Liu, J., Mustanski, B., Dick, D., Bolland, J., & Kertes, D. A. (2017). Risk and protective factors for comorbid internalizing and externalizing problems among economically disadvantaged African American youth. *Development and Psychopathology, 29*(3), 1043–1056. doi:10.1017/S0954579416001012

Lund, C., Brooke-Sumner, C., Baingana, F., Baron, E. C., Breuer, E., Chandra, P., . . . Saxena, S. (2018). Social determinants of mental disorders and the sustainable development goals: A systematic review of reviews. *Lancet Psychiatry, 5*(4), 357–369. doi:10.1016/S2215–0366(18)30060–9

Luyten, P., Campbell, C., Allison, E., & Fonagy, P. (2020). The mentalizing approach to psychopathology: State of the art and future directions. *Annual Review of Clinical Psychology, 16*, 297–325. doi:10.1146/annurev-clinpsy-071919–015355

Lyons-Ruth, K. (1998). Implicit relational knowing: Its role in development and psychoanalytic treatment. *Infant Mental Health Journal, 7*, 127–131.

Lyons-Ruth, K. (1999). The two person unconscious: Intersubjective dialogue, enactive relational representation and the emergence of new forms of relational organisation. *Psychoanalytic Inquiry, 19*(4), 576–617.

Mahler, M. S., & Gosliner, J. (1955). On symbiotic child psychosis: genetic, dynamic and restitutive aspects. *Psychoanalytic Study of the Child, 10*, 195–212.

Marks, M. (2002). Letting fathers in. In J. Trowell (Ed.), *The importance of fathers: A psychoanalytic re-evaluation* (pp. 93–106). Hove: Brunner-Routledge.

McDougall, J. (1989). *Theatres of the body.* London: Free Association Books.

Meltzoff, A. N., & Moore, M. K. (1998). Infant intersubjectivity: Broadening the dialogue to include imitation, identity and intention. In S. Braten (Ed.), *Intersubjective communication and emotion in early ontogeny* (pp. 47–62). Paris: Cambridge University Press.

Paquette, D. (2004). Dichotomizing paternal and maternal functions as a means to better understand their primary contributions. *Human Development, 47*(4). doi:10.1159/000078726

Pederson, D. R., Moran, G., Sitko, C., Campbell, K., Ghesquire, K., & Acton, H. (1990). Maternal sensitivity and the security of infant-mother attachment: A Q-sort study. *Child Development, 61*(6), 1974–1983. doi:10.1111/j.1467–8624.1990. tb03579.x. PMID: 2083509

Richter, L. (2010). Global perspectives on the well-being of children. In C. Worthman, P. M. Plotsky, D. S. Schechter, & C. A. Cummings (Eds.), *Formative experiences: The interactions of caregiving, culture and developmental psychbiology* (pp. 531–548). Cambridge: Cambridge University Press.

Saffran, J. R., & Kirkham, N. Z. (2018). Infant statistical learning. *Annual Review of Psychology, 69*, 181–203. doi:10.1146/annurev-psych-122216–011805

Stern, D. N. (1985). *The interpersonal world of the infant: A view from psychoanalysis and developmental psychology.* New York, NY: Basic Books.

Stern, D. N. (1998). The process of therapeutic change involving implicit knowledge: Some implications of developmental observations for adult psychotherapy. *Infant Mental Health Journal, 19*, 300–308.

Stern, D. N. (2010). *The present moment in psychotherapy and everyday life.* London: W. W. Norton.

Target, M., & Fonagy, P. (2002). Fathers in modern psychoanalysis and in society: The role of the father and child development. In J. Trowell (Ed.), *The importance of fathers: A psychoanalytic re-evaluation* (pp. 41–60). Hove: Brunner-Routledge.

Trevarthen, C., & Aitken, K. J. (2001). Infant intersubjectivity: Research, theory, and clinical applications. *Journal of Child Psychology and Psychiatry, 42,* 3–48.

Tronick, E. (1989). Emotions and emotional communication in infants. *American Psychologist, 44*(2), 112–119.

Trowell, J. (2002). Setting the scene. In J. Trowell (Ed.), *The importance of fathers: A psychoanalytic re-evaluation* (pp. 3–19). Hove: Brunner-Routledge.

Verhage, M. L., Schuengel, C., Madigan, S., Fearon, R. M., Oosterman, M., Cassibba, R., . . . van IJzendoorn, M. H. (2016). Narrowing the transmission gap: A synthesis of three decades of research on intergenerational transmission of attachment. *Psychological Bulletin, 142*(4), 337–366. doi:10.1037/bul0000038

von Klitzing, K. (2019). The role fathers in early child development. In *Working with fathers in psychoanalytic parent-infant psychotherapy.* London: Routledge.

von Klitzing, K., Simoni, H., Amsler, F., & Bürgin, D. (1999). The role of the father in early family interactions. *Infant Mental Health Journal, 20*(3), 222–237.

von Klitzing, K., & Stadelmann, S. (2011). Das Kind in der triadischen Beziehungswelt. *Psyche, 65*(9), 953–972.

Winnicott, D. W. (1960). The theory of the parent-infant relationship. *International Journal of Psycho-Analysis, 41,* 585–595.

Winnicott, D. W. (2016a). The ordinary devoted mother and her baby: Nine broadcast talks. In L. Caldwell & H. Taylor Robinson (Eds.), *The collected works of D. W. Winnicott: Volume 7, 1964–1966.* Oxford: Oxford University Press.

Winnicott, D. W. (2016b). The relationship of a mother to her baby at the beginning. In L. Caldwell & H. Taylor Robinson (Eds.), *The collected works of D. W. Winnicott.* Oxford: Oxford University Press.

3   Trauma in the parent-infant relationship

A minority of parents relate to their babies in ways that constitute an adverse relational environment for development. In extremis, they may either not protect their baby from outside stresses or may even be the source of stress for the baby. In relational environments that are traumatizing for the baby, the likelihood of the baby's development being compromised is higher. We will consider the two sides of the coin: the parent's traumatic experience of parenting their young baby, and the baby's experience of traumatization.

Trauma appears to infiltrate the parent-infant relationship and impact the infant via the traumatized state of mind of the parent. The circumstances may be the occurrence of a single traumatic event or series of events which overwhelm the parent to the extent that they are unable to buffer their infant from the stress. Homelessness, forced migration and bereavement are examples of situations where a parent may be too flooded by anxiety, fear, grief etc., to genuinely attend to their baby. Another source of trauma, often unconscious and unintentional, lies in the parent's mind and ways of relating to the baby. Schore has termed this "relational trauma" to describe those situations where traumatogenic experiences happen within the ordinary transactions between parent and baby in the course of looking after the baby (Schore, 2000). In both forms of trauma, the consequence is that the baby may be left in prolonged, overwhelming states of negative affect without adult comfort. This has been described as "toxic stress" because of its potential to cumulatively impact the architecture of the developing brain (National Scientific Council on the Developing Child, 2014).

The dilemma of the baby whose love object/attachment figure is also the source of threat to his integrity has been described as "fright without solution" (Hesse & Main, 1999, p. 484). In such situations, "the infant perpetually experiences arousal of attachment needs [authors' clarification: i.e., the need to be close to a protective, safety – providing

DOI: 10.4324/9781003024323-3

attachment figure] without receiving the comfort and soothing to termi-
nate them" (Madigan et al., 2006, p. 192).

What does a baby feel when his mother is empty of love, or when he
nearly died at birth, or when his mother nearly died in the act of birthing
him? Perhaps because to think of such distress in a young infant is in itself
so disturbing, it has been psychoanalytic-informed thinkers – trained as
they are to acknowledge those aspects of experience that we normally
avoid thinking about – who have most astutely described such states.
One of the insights of psychoanalytic thinking has been to describe how
emotional trauma might be experienced by an infant as an overwhelming fear of disintegration and death. This is rooted in, and the expression of, the condition of infantile helplessness and dependency on his
parent/parents for physical and psychological survival. Winnicott coined
the phrase "unthinkable anxiety" – an experience characterized by sensations such as "going to pieces" or "falling forever" (Winnicott, 1962,
p. 58). Bion, who worked extensively with states of trauma, described
the experience of existential disaster for the infant, when the parental
mind is unable to receive and work with her baby's raw emotions, as
"nameless dread" (Bion, 1962, p. 308). Beebe suggests that the infant is
left confused "about their own basic emotional organization, about their
mothers' emotional organization, and about their mothers' response to
their distress, setting a trajectory in development which may disturb the
fundamental integration of the person" (Beebe et al., 2010, p. 3).

Adaptation and defence

In thinking about how relational trauma can impinge on development,
we need to think about the different ways an infant can try to respond,
or rather adapt to, to these experiences. In psychoanalytic terms, these
adaptations (which occur not only in babies) are described as defences:
mental mechanisms which keep painful, frightening, conflictual feelings
and ideas out of awareness. The infant will use defences to preserve the
integrity of his or her very being in the face of threat. Early emerging
defences were identified by infant clinicians such as Spitz (Spitz, 1961),
Fraiberg (Fraiberg, 1982) and Winnicott (Winnicott, 1960) and have
been explored in more recent neuropsychological and attachment work
by researchers such as Perry (Perry, 1997), Panskepp (Panksepp, 2001)
and Schore (Schore, 2003). Very early defences include withdrawal,
avoidance, hyper-vigilance, dissociation and freezing (playing dead).
Although adaptive in the circumstance of their immediate needs in
infancy, such defences may in the longer-term become entrenched, maladaptive ways of being in the social world.

Attachment theory provides another framework for understanding how these processes emerge and shape development, via the concept of disorganized attachment. Bowlby's attachment theory originally identified three categories of attachment style: secure, avoidant and anxious. Later, the pre-eminent attachment researcher, Mary Main, and colleagues, proposed a fourth category – disorganized (Main & Hesse, 1990b; Main & Solomon, 1986). This category was introduced in response to the presence of a small subgroup whose behaviour in the "strange situation procedure" did not fall into any of the original three categories. The Strange Situation is a method developed by Ainsworth, in which young children's responses to separation and reunification with their parent are observed and rated in terms of attachment style. The disorganized subgroup exhibited fearful, contradictory and/or disoriented behaviours, such as stereotypies, freezing and approaching and retreating from their parent on reunion.

It is important to note that disorganized attachment is not itself a disorder, does not reliably suggest maltreatment and not all infants who are rated as disorganized develop later difficulties (Granqvist et al., 2017). Further, attachment styles are not fixed traits. However, despite the need for caution in its application, the concept of disorganized attachment can be useful to the PPIP therapist when it comes to understanding the experience of an infant, who has repeatedly found their parents to be a source of alarm. This has been supported by research observing the behaviours of parents of infants rated as disorganized, which have been identified as hostile, fearful, dissociated and withdrawal behaviours in the parent in response to infant cues. These behaviours can be quite subtle, fleeting and outside the parent's awareness:

> "Frightening and anomalous" behaviours on the part of the parent are often performed unconsciously when interacting with or tending to an infant whilst unresolved feelings of loss or trauma in relation to their own attachment experiences wash over the parent.
>
> (Hesse & Main, 2000)

Disorganization is assumed to indicate a lack of coherent defence in the infant and is associated with disruption and unpredictability in the parent-infant relationship, particularly in circumstances of high arousal. In such circumstances, aspects of the interactive coordination between parent and infant are significantly lowered (Beebe & Lachmann, 2014). The parents' difficulty in coordinating interactions and joining affectively with the infant results in the baby feeling incoherent and destabilized and unable to influence the emotional trajectory with their parent (Hobson, 2002).

Co-construction of defences as modes of relating

Often defensive patterns of behaviour in the infant emerge in tandem with the parent's own adaptations to their social environment. The impact of trauma as a one-off event has been shown in the example of Beatrice Beebe and colleagues' work with a group of pregnant women who lost their partners in the 9/11 destruction of the Twin Towers in New York. The researchers studied how the effects of maternal trauma got titrated into the mother-infant interactions (Beebe et al., 2020). It was found that many of the 9/11 widows and babies worked hard to maintain positive affect and immediately repair any negative interactions: "A vigilant, hyper-contingent, high-arousal engagement was the central mode of the interpersonal transmission of the trauma to these infants" (Beebe et al., 2020, p. 1). As the authors suggest, this pattern of vigilant engagement may have been adaptive at the time and constitute resilience – an attempt by mothers to override their distress and to protect themselves and their infants from overwhelming sadness and fear. What we may learn from such detailed data on the interactions between the mothers and infants in this sample is the sensitivity and adaptiveness of the infants' responses and communications, and the poignancy of the way in which both mother and infant seek to respond to each other's needs and to protect each other and their relationship. As Beebe and colleagues discuss, however, there are risks in such adaptations – the vigilant, hyper-aroused nature of the engagement can transmit to the infant a sense of trauma through the "emergency mode" such functioning generates, and the risk may arise that the infant's other developmental tasks, such as learning to explore the world and develop a separate sense of themselves in the world, may be inhibited by the imperative to maintain hyper-engagement. We use this example of an empirical study of the impact of a catastrophic one-off trauma because it captures so eloquently the way in which trauma can reverberate through relational lines.

Transgenerational patterns and mechanisms of transmission

Why do some parents, often across generations, respond to their infants in ways that impinge so sharply on their infants' self-experience? A key concept in psychoanalysis is the "repetition compulsion", which applies to the re-enactment of painful situations and feelings from the person's past (Freud, 1914). The mechanisms that underpin repetition are repression and dissociation: these function to keep separate the memory of the events and the affects, the feelings, associated with it. Dissociation is an adaptive mechanism because pain is not felt. Consequently, the past is fundamentally unremembered in a meaningful way and the individual is unable to make sense of it or to recognize its repetition in their present life.

Fraiberg and colleagues applied this idea to explain intergenerational repetitions of adverse parenting: traumatic events and feelings from the past, coined "ghosts in the nursery", are unconsciously re-enacted in the parent's relationship with the baby (Fraiberg, Adelson, & Shapiro, 1975). The "ghosts" are "visitors from the unremembered past of the parents" (i.e., a past to which the mechanism of dissociation has been applied), whose invasion condemns the parent "to repeat the tragedy of his childhood with his baby in terrible and exacting detail". Thus, "a parent and his child may find themselves re-enacting a moment or a scene from another time with another set of characters" (Fraiberg et al., 1975, p. 388). A classic example described by Fraiberg is of a mother who could not hear her baby's cries until her own unheeded infantile cries – her "ghosts" – were heard and put to rest through the therapy. The therapy provided an emotionally safe environment in which the infantile pain that the mother had carried within her could become conscious, and the mother's state of mind in relation to her childhood was transformed from inchoate to psychologically meaningful (Fraiberg, 1980). An example from our clinical practice is a mother who presented her 1-month-old child as a vampire: greedy and depleting. Her descriptions of the baby were replete with statements such as: "dealing with him is like dealing with bailiffs . . . he eats me up to the last crumb . . . I am tired, tired, tired, how much more does he want?" In this statement, the mother was expressing that she did not see her baby for who he was in age, capacities, intentions but rather as a powerful person whose personality traits persecuted and victimized her. When asked who she is reminded of, she replied: "I don't see nothing of myself in him, I see his father. He has that look, you know, he has his look". Exploring further, mother disclosed that she felt that her own mother had the same kind of look. In other words, this baby was the object of the mother's negative transference, from her own mother when she was an infant, via her partner, to the baby. Part of the struggle was, therefore, to combat the control she felt the baby had over her.

This mother was harsh not only in her descriptions of her baby; the therapist observed that she was also unsympathetic in her treatment of him, for example, laughing lightly when he cried. This seemingly surprising behaviour highlights another psychological defence that can come into play in the transmission of relational trauma – that of identification with the aggressor. As described by Anna Freud, this defence enables the individual to (unconsciously) switch from experiencing the victim's feelings of fear and helplessness to those of the aggressor/abuser's power and control (Freud, 1936). Within the parent-infant relationship, unconsciously the threat may be that the baby's infantile state of needy helplessness and raw emotion will re-evoke deeply buried states of helplessness within the parent. Raphael-Leff has described this phenomenon as "contagious arousal" – re-activated anxieties related to the weakest links of the parent's own infantile experience (Raphael-Leff, 2003). Identification with the aggressor then reverses the power-dynamic that threatens to break down their psychic functioning.

The mother's depiction of her 1-month baby as a "bailiff" and a "vampire" raises the issue of parental representations: conscious and unconscious feelings, fantasies, expectations and projections which influence the parent's experience of, and attitude towards, his or her child. While the parent's representations reflect current circumstances around the conception, birth and parenting of the particular baby, they are also influenced by their own attachment representations derived in infancy (van IJzendoorn, 1995). The mother in this example was beset with aggrieved memories of her own mother's cruelty towards her as a small child, which seemed to be transferred onto her baby. We may also ask about the bailiff/vampire aspects of herself that seemed to be projected onto her baby. Is the mother also communicating that she has such needy, devouring and retributive feelings in herself that are intolerable to hold within? Are these now deposited in to the baby, but also coming back to haunt her – as projections tend to? A wish to repress the hungry baby inside was expressed in this mother's severe attitude towards her food consumption, which was strictly limited to "only healthy food, and in small quantities".

From a mentalizing point of view, in this illustration, the mother's view of what the baby's look communicated was fixed: there were no other perspectives, no possibility that her baby's look could convey different meanings at different times or that there could be other ways of thinking about what her infant might be feeling. Furthermore, she was not able to adjust to the feedback from her baby. For example, when her baby continued to fret, it was taken as a reflection of his obstinacy. Another mother, with greater reflective capacities, may have wondered whether her baby was still unsettled because she had misunderstood what was bothering him/her in the first instance and whether some other response was needed. Mentalizing does not only involve abstract thoughts and beliefs; the embodied nature of mentalizing is perhaps particularly relevant to the care of young children (Fotopoulou & Tsakiris, 2017). The way in which mental state reasoning does not operate in isolation from other kinds of responses is indicated in the research finding that frequent non-attuned references to the infant's mental states were associated with touch behaviours that were not contingent with the infant's feelings. The authors suggest that "when parental high-order social cognitive abilities [authors' comment: including mentalizing] are compromised, they are also likely to translate into inappropriate, tactile attempts to regulate infant's emotions" (Crucianelli et al., 2019, p. 1). This eventually led to fewer affective tactile responses from the infant, which suggests to us that the infants experienced the non-contingent touch as unpleasurable, and possibly withdrew from seeking a mentalizing object in their physical contact with their parents.

Mechanisms of transmission

Developmental researchers such as Main and Hesse (Main & Hesse, 1990a, 1990b), Lyons-Ruth (Lyons-Ruth & Jacobvitz, 2008a, 2008b), Madigan (Madigan et al., 2006) and Beebe (Beebe et al., 2010) have tried to identify the micro-mechanisms through which the parent's state of mind might traumatize the baby. They describe behavioural changes in a parent in whom disturbing unconscious material breaks through so that the parent is suddenly flooded by internal sensations, memories and affects that have been vigorously defended against. In a state of anxiety and fright themselves when the repressed material breaks through, anomalous behaviours may be displayed by the parent in interactions with their infants. The parent may be unaware that they are displaying these behaviours and they will appear inexplicable from the infant's point of view. The behaviours may be "frightened, threatening, and dissociative" (Main & Hesse, 1990b); extremely insensitive behaviours which fail to soothe the infant's distressed arousal (Lyons-Ruth, Bronfman, and Parsons, 1999); inaccessibility of the parent as a figure of comfort and safety – as when withdrawn, depressed (Solomon & George, 1999); or, when s/he reacts to the infant's expressions of emotions inappropriately (Lyons-Ruth & Jacobvitz, 1999) (as in the case of the mother described earlier who laughed anxiously and helplessly when her baby cried). In such a scenario, the parent is unable to mentalize themselves or their baby. From the baby's perspective, it may be adaptive to switch off the emergent possibility of making sense of their parent – because the parent's mental state may be too frightening or aversive for the baby to consider. A brief video clip of a baby being pushed on a swing in a playground showed the mother smiling at her baby as she pushed the swing in front of her. It was surprising to see the baby avoiding this face-to-face interaction, and instead turning his head sharply to the side. Frame-by-frame analysis showed that the mother's facial expression (eyes, muscular tonality) was not matched to a smile; a fleeting baring of the teeth suggested that it was in fact a grimace. The baby would have experienced the grimace at a bodily level and understood the threat therein.

Repeated experiences of fright may accrue into a disorganized attachment pattern, which expresses the infant's inability to develop a coherent defensive blueprint in the face of his or her cumulative experience of extreme, unpredictable and incomprehensible parental lability. Neuroscientists speak of alterations in certain neurocognitive systems which "may reflect calibration to early risk environments" (McCrory & Viding, 2015, p. 493), and we are here describing the developmental distortion of the infant's attachment system to accommodate relational trauma in order to survive psychologically. Unfortunately, we may then anticipate a circular feedback loop of negative emotions and expectations between parent and baby. For example, the infant who turns away from his parent – when the parent is *unaware* that s/he is frightening the baby – can be easily experienced by the parent as a rejecting or hostile baby. The sense of "my baby doesn't love me" is painful and shaming and may evoke more withdrawal, hostility or aggression in the parent.

References

Beebe, B., Hoven, C. W., Kaitz, M., Steele, M., Musa, G., Margolis, A., Ewing, J., Sossin, M., & Lee, S. H. (2020). Urgent engagement in 9/11 pregnant widows and their infants: Transmission of trauma. *Infancy*, *25*(2). doi:10.1111/infa.12323

Beebe, B., Jaffe, J., Markese, S., Buck, K., Chen, H., Cohen, P., . . . Feldstein, S. (2010). The origins of 12-month attachment: A microanalysis of 4-month mother-infant interaction. *Attachment and Human Development*, *12*(1–2), 3–141. doi:10.1080/14616730903338985

Beebe, B., & Lachmann, F. M. (2014). *The origins of attachment: Infant research and adult treatment*. New York, NY: Routledge.

Bion, W. R. (1962). The psycho-analytic study of thinking. *International Journal of Psychoanalysis*, *43*, 306–310.

Crucianelli, L., Wheatley, L., Filippetti, M. L., Jenkinson, P. M., Kirk, E., & Fotopoulou, A. K. (2019). The mindedness of maternal touch: An investigation of maternal mind-mindedness and mother-infant touch interactions. *Developmental Cognitive Neuroscience*, *35*, 47–56. doi:10.1016/j.dcn.2018.01.010

Fotopoulou, A., & Tsakiris, M. (2017). Mentalizing homeostasis: The social origins of interoceptive inference. *Neuropsychoanalysis*, *19*(1), 3–28. doi:10.1080/1529414 5.2017.1294031

Fraiberg, S. (1980). *Clinical studies in infant mental health: The first year of life*. New York, NY: Basic Books.

Fraiberg, S. (1982). Pathological defenses in infancy. *Psychoanalytic Quarterly*, *51*(4), 612–635.

Fraiberg, S., Adelson, E., & Shapiro, V. (1975). Ghosts in the nursery: A psychoanalytic approach to the problems of impaired infant-mother relationships. *Journal of the American Academy of Child Psychiatry, 14*(3), 387–421.

Freud, A. (1936). *The ego and the mechanisms of defence.* New York, NY: International Universities Press, 1946.

Freud, S. (1914). Remembering, repeating, and working through. In J. Strachey (Ed.), *The standard edition of the complete psychological works of Sigmund Freud* (Vol. 12, pp. 145–156). London, UK: Hogarth Press, 1958.

Granqvist, P., Sroufe, L. A., Dozier, M., Hesse, E., Steele, M., van Ijzendoorn, M., . . . Duschinsky, R. (2017). Disorganized attachment in infancy: A review of the phenomenon and its implications for clinicians and policy-makers. *Attachment and Human Development, 19*(6), 534–558. doi:10.1080/14616734.2017.1354040

Hesse, E., & Main, M. (1999). Second-generation effects of unresolved trauma in nonmaltreating parents: Dissociated, frightened, and threatening parental behavior. *Psychoanalytic Inquiry, 19*(4), 481–540. doi:10.1080/07351699909534265

Hesse, E., & Main, M. (2000). Disorganized infant, child, and adult attachment: Collapse in behavioral and attentional strategies. *Journal of the American Psychoanalytic Association, 48*(4), 1097–1127.

Hobson, P. (2002). *The cradle of thought: Explorations of the origins of thinking.* Oxford, UK: Macmillan.

Lyons-Ruth, K., Bronfman, E., & Parsons, E. (1999). Atypical attachment in infancy and early childhood among children at developmental risk. IV. Maternal frightened, frightening, or atypical behavior and disorganized infant attachment patterns. *Monographs of the Society for Research in Child Development, 64*(3), 67–96. doi:10.1111/1540-5834.0003

Lyons-Ruth, K., & Jacobovitz, D. (1999). Attachment disorganization: Unresolved loss, relational violence and lapses in behavioral and attentional strategies. In J. Cassidy & P. R. Shaver (Eds.), *Handbook of attachment theory and research* (pp. 520–554). New York: Guilford.

Lyons-Ruth, K., & Jacobvitz, D. (2008a). Attachment disorganization: Genetic factors, parenting contexts, and developmental transformation from infancy to adulthood. In J. Cassidy & P. R. Shaver (Eds.), *Handbook of attachment: Theory, research, and clinical applications* (2nd ed., pp. 666–697). New York, NY: Guilford Press.

Lyons-Ruth, K., & Jacobvitz, D. (2008b). Attachment disorganization: Unresolved loss, relational violence, and lapses in behavioral and attentional strategies. In J. Cassidy & P. R. Shaver (Eds.), *Handbook of attachment: Theory, research and clinical applications* (2nd ed., pp. 520–554). New York: Guilford.

Madigan, S., Bakermans-Kranenburg, M. J., Van Ijzendoorn, M. H., Moran, G., Pederson, D. R., & Benoit, D. (2006). Unresolved states of mind, anomalous parental behavior, and disorganized attachment: A review and meta-analysis of a transmission gap. *Attachment and Human Development, 8*(2), 89–111. doi:10.1080/14616730600774458

Main, M., & Hesse, E. (1990a). The insecure disorganized/disoriented attachment pattern in infancy: Precursors and sequelae. In M. Greenberg, D. Cicchetti, & E. M. Cummings (Eds.), *Attachment in the preschool years: Theory, research, and intervention* (pp. 161–182). Chicago, IL: University Chicago Press.

Main, M., & Hesse, E. (1990b). Parents' unresolved traumatic experiences are related to infant disorganized attachment status: Is frightened and/or frightening parental behavior the linking mechanism? In M. T. Greenberg, D. Cicchetti, & E. M. Cummings (Eds.), *Attachment in the preschool years: Theory, research and intervention* (pp. 161–182). Chicago, IL: University of Chicago Press.

Main, M., & Solomon, J. (1986). Discovery of an insecure-disorganized/disoriented attachment pattern. In T. B. Brazelton & M. W. Yogman (Eds.), *Affective development in infancy* (pp. 95–124). Norwood, NJ: Ablex.

McCrory, E., & Viding, E. (2015). The theory of latent vulnerability: Reconceptualizing the link between childhood maltreatment and psychiatric disorder. *Development and Psychopathology, 27*(2), 493–505. doi:10.1017/S0954579415000115

National Scientific Council on the Developing Child. (2005/2014). *Excessive stress disrupts the architecture of the developing brain: Working Paper 3.* Updated Edition. http://www.developingchild.harvard.edu

Panksepp, J. (2001). The long-term psychobiological consequences of infant emotions: Prescriptions for the twenty-first century. *Infant Mental Health Journal, 22*(1–2), 132–173.

Perry, B. (1997). Incubated in terror: Neurodevelopmental factors in the "cycle of violence". In J. Osofsky (Ed.), *Children in a violent society* (pp. 124–149). New York, NY: Guilford Press.

Raphael-Leff, J. (2003). Treatment for perinatal disturbance. *Journal of Child and Adolescent Mental Health, 15*(1), 49–53. doi:10.2989/17280580309486541

Schore, A. N. (2000). *Early relational trauma and the development of the right brain: Unpublished invited presentation.* London: Anna Freud Centre.

Schore, A. N. (2003). *Affect regulation and the repair of the self.* New York: Norton.

Solomon, J., & George, C. (1999). *Attachment disorganization.* New York: Guilford.

Spitz, R. A. (1961). Some early prototypes of ego defenses. *Journal of the American Psychoanalytic Association, 9*(4), 626–651.

van IJzendoorn, M. H. (1995). Adult attachment representations, parental responsiveness, and infant attachment: A meta-analysis on the predictive validity of the Adult Attachment Interview. *Psychological Bulletin, 117*(3), 387–403. doi:10.1037/0033–2909.117.3.387

Winnicott, D. W. (1960). The theory of the parent-infant relationship. *International Journal of Psycho-Analysis, 41*, 585–595.

Winnicott, D. W. (1962). Ego integration in child development. In D. W. Winnicott (Ed.), *The maturational processes and the facilitating environment* (pp. 56–63). London: Hogarth Press, 1965.

4   Parent–infant psychotherapy

Parent-infant psychotherapy evolved as a defined treatment modality in the 1960s and 1970s to address the specific clinical phenomena of compromised interactions between parent and infant that may negatively impact the infant's development. The overarching purpose of parent-infant psychotherapy is to support the development of both infant and parent via their relationship. The Cochrane Report on parent-infant psychotherapy summarizes it as follows:

> Parent-infant psychotherapy is intended to address problems in the parent-infant relationship, and problems such as excessive crying and sleeping/eating difficulties. A parent-infant psychotherapist works directly with the parent and infant in the home or clinic, to identify unconscious patterns of relating and behaving, and influences from the past that are impeding the parent-infant relationship. . . . The intervention is delivered to individual dyads but can also be delivered to small groups of parents and infants.
> (Barlow, Bennett, Midgley, Larkin, & Wei, 2015, p. 3)

Parent-infant psychotherapy originally reflected the dominant mother-centric theories of child development and the historical socio-economic, cultural, and research contexts in which these ideas were embedded. The psychoanalytic orientation of the modality was introduced by early pioneers such as psychoanalysts Selma Fraiberg and her colleagues at the University of California, USA, Serge Lebovici and colleagues at the Centre Alfred Binet in Paris, and Cramer, Brazelton and colleagues in Geneva.

The following quotations illuminate the complex early thinking of these psychoanalytic parent-infant psychotherapy innovators. Paediatrician, psychiatrist and psychoanalyst Serge Lebovici wrote about the transgenerational inner world of parenting in a family:

DOI: 10.4324/9781003024323-4

Having a child does not mean that one is its parent: the path leading to parenthood" assumes that" we have "co-constructed" with our child and the latter's grandparents a "tree of life" which testifies to intergenerational transmission and the existence of a double process of parenting-filiation thanks to which parents can become father and mother. Considering parenthood today means accepting that this human phenomenon involves the interweaving of biological, psychological and cultural elements. This is a notion that contains a paradox, since it is both natural biologically and from the point of view of social organization, but also extremely complex psychically and culturally. Basically, this is a transgenerational process at the origin of human beings [authors' translation].

(Solis-Ponton, 2001)

Psychiatrist and psychoanalyst Bertrand Cramer wrote about non-conscious processes of transmission in the day-to-day care of the child:

It's simple. I innovated in the field of mother-baby therapies by focusing on the daily trade of mothers with their children. I have studied how adults imprint messages and values on the soul of the child, most often without their knowledge. This interaction has two facets. The first appears during discussions around food, bathing, bedtime. The video makes it possible to capture these gestures, these attitudes which are as important as the spoken word. The second is an imaginary, phantasmic world that is revealed during interviews, for example, when a patient tells that the child she rejects reminds her of her own father who was a violent man.

(Cramer, 1999)

Psychiatrist and child psychoanalyst Selma Fraiberg describes the role of the baby as an agent for change in the parent:

The baby can be a catalyst. He provides a powerful motive for positive change in his parents. He represents their hopes and deepest longings; he stands for renewal of the self; his birth can be experienced as a psychological rebirth for his parents. The baby, in fact, evokes profound memories and feelings in his parents which normally lie deep in the personality. This need not lead to pathological disturbance. To be in touch with the deepest reservoirs of feeling in oneself can lead to a binding together of the elements of personality, a form of self-healing. When the stirring of old conflicts does lead to grave disturbance in the parents (as we see in many of our patients), we find we are still advantaged in our work. The powerful conflicts that have led to this crisis have broken through into consciousness, or near consciousness, ready, as it were, for our help in resolution and healing – perhaps more ready that at any other time in adult life.

(Fraiberg, 1980, pp. 53–54)

However, just as PPIP was limited by a mother-centric viewpoint, it has also been dominated by a western middle-class perspective on healthy childhood and development. It is only in recent years that this cultural view has been challenged to be inclusive of broader cultural theories of development and disturbance. Thus, for example, perinatal work in deprived populations has highlighted the extent to which differences in race, language, education, socio-economic status and culture can create divergences between therapist and patient perceptions of what is a "compromised interaction". Consider differing attitudes of parents towards preparing their infant for life: a mother of a 6-month-old baby, for example, sees him crawl towards a potentially painful but not dangerous source of heat. For some parents, a protective response would be to remove the baby and explain that the object is hot and could hurt them. For other parents, preparing the child for life would involve exposing the child to such threats to support self-learning about adversity. The therapist may wonder whether intergenerational trauma is possibly being enacted, or that mother has entered a dissociative state. What also needs to be borne in mind is that a history of state violence towards its citizens, and violence within the community towards women and children, may have been translated into a parenting tradition of letting the child "learn the hard way" in preparation for survival in a harsh world. Thus, while bequeathed a very rich body of knowledge, parent-infant psychotherapy, and perhaps particularly psychoanalytic PIP, has also had much to review and revise in relation to its own traditions, and needs to keep this iterative process alive.

In undertaking PPIP, parents commit to a process of self-enquiry that may be outside their life experiences. As Fraiberg wrote:

We need trust in order to do our work, but the largest number of our parents have not known trust in their own childhood experiences with parents and parent figures . . . We need a strong a strong desire from our families to be "good parents", but many of them have no models of good parenting on which to build. We need from them a wish to change . . . however, the majority of our parents, when they first come to us, do not see change as a product of self -observation and personal growth . . . Most of our patients do not come with the "self-motivation" that is so highly valued in psychotherapy.

(Fraiberg, 1980, p. 28)

Fraiberg argues that the motivational basis for a parent to participate in PPIP is the wish to do best for their baby. This is our experience too. For example, it is the wish to better than what they had themselves that can keep a parent going through painful mourning of the parenting they did not receive, or to persist in attending sessions when the going feels too slow.

The model of parent-infant psychotherapy developed at the Anna Freud Centre

History

In 1997, the Anna Freud Centre received a government Health Innovation, Excellence and Service Development Award to develop and deliver parent-infant psychotherapy and to train allied professionals in this to-be-developed and evaluated model of early intervention. The evolving model of parent-infant psychotherapy drew on core psychoanalytic ideas about the nature of parenting and child development. Thus, from the beginning, the PPIP model, manualized in 2005 (Baradon & Broughton, Gibbs, James, Joyce & Woodhead 2005) and revised in 2016 (Baradon & Biseo, Broughton, James, & Joyce, 2016), has been a form of applied psychoanalysis with an Anna Freudian theoretical framework regarding normative development and earliest relational disturbance. Over time, a pivotal discussion has evolved regarding how, and to what extent, socio-economic, societal and cultural factors may change the definition of "normative" in any given period.

Anna Freud's legacy in PPIP

In this section we shall discuss some of the ways in which the thinking of Anna Freud, daughter of Sigmund and founder of the Hampstead Child Therapy Course and Clinic (renamed the Anna Freud Centre after her death in 1982), has influenced PPIP (for an excellent overview of Anna Freud's work, see Midgley, 2012). Anna Freud published extensively; the ideas that have particularly influenced PPIP are elaborated in three key publications. The first of these was *The Ego and Mechanisms of Defence* which, based on extensive clinical evidence, describes the ways and means by which the ego wards off unpleasure and anxiety, and exercises control over impulsive behaviour, affects and instinctive urges (Freud, 1936). In PPIP we observe how habitual defences may infiltrate a parent's interactions with their infant and infant defences are co-constructed with their parent. Furthermore, parent and infant defences shape the therapeutic relationship and clinical process. During the Second World War, Anna Freud and Dorothy Burlingham published *Infants without Families: The Case for and against Residential Nurseries* (Freud & Burlingham, 1944), which describes their experience with children dealing with separation, bereavement and displacement in the Hampstead War Nursery during the war. This book laid the basis for the methodological approach of observation and the collation of observational resources in thinking about the individual infant and family, and in understanding the importance of the granular impact of daily familial transactions for the young child. Finally, *Normality and Pathology* reconceptualizes the developmental process itself and introduces the idea of childhood difficulties as "disorders of development" (Freud, 1965). This has been central to our understanding of arrests and deviations in the development of our infant patients.

The child's experience

Perhaps the fundamental shaping principle of Anna Freud's approach is her interest in and engagement with the minds of children. As Goldstein wrote:

> Miss Freud taught us to put childish things before, not behind, us. She taught us to place ourselves in a child's skin, to try to think a child's thoughts and feel a child's feelings about being "removed from a known environment to an unknown one". . . . She helped us understand that a child, like an adult, is "a person in his own right"; but that unlike an adult, he "changes constantly from one state of growth to another," measuring the passage of time not by clock and calendar but by his "own built in time sense, based on the urgency of [his] instinctual and emotional needs".
> (Goldstein, 1982, pp. 221–222)

The attempt to enter imaginatively into the experience of the non-verbal and as yet non-symbolizing baby is a unique aspect of PPIP. In many ways, babies' subjectivity has been unchartered territory for many years; even today infant sentience is not universally accepted by parents or practitioners, and nor has a language been developed for it. In PPIP, the "language" that has been developed hovers on the boundaries of soma and psyche. Imaginings of the therapist will include embodied emotional experiences, such as "Does that loud voice hurt in your heart or your tummy? Did you get a fright there?" Such attempts to find ways to understand the experience of the baby can be thought of as mentalizing the infant, which is now understood as a key process in helping the infant develop a sense of self and agency. The work of developmental scientists, for example Gergely, has further increased our awareness of the social awareness and sophistication of infants, for example, their sensitivity to whether others are behaving with intentionality and appear to be wishing to communicate interactively (Tauzin & Gergely, 2019).

Observation

Anna Freud established observation as a form of "action research" to study the psychological functioning of an individual child and – when collated and organized across many individuals – as a methodology for creating a body of knowledge to inform the field of child development (Midgley, 2007). This was developed out of her own experience of encouraging her staff in the Hampstead War Nurseries to make detailed observations of all aspects of the lives of the children in their care, which could then be brought together to study the development of each child, as well as topics of interest (such as reactions to separation) on a cross-case basis. Observation is the process of recording the moment-to-moment behaviours, activities, responses and expressions of the subject over a set period of time. Observation continues to be part and parcel of the PPIP approach to get to know the baby, the parents and their relationship. It is integral to the reflective stance of the therapist, and it is associated with the capacity to take a mental pause in the midst of the melee of a session, to touch base with what is unfolding in the moment. The principle of observation has also been taken a step further by recording sessions on video and viewing the videos in the team as part of the clinical discussion of the families in treatment. We have found that watching videos of sessions is one of the major tools for learning and reflectivity. Not only does it provide for greater understanding of patient material, often through repeated viewing of puzzling interactions, but it hones the therapist's skills of observation, enables a clearer distinction between observation and interpretation of what has been observed, and informs the therapist about her own non-conscious actions and communications in the session. The microanalysis of a case study, described in Chapter 7, describes how this observational work has been expanded and developed via the microanalytic technique.

Child psychology and developmental disturbance

The working model of infants' "developmental psychology" and "developmental disturbance" embedded in PPIP is inherently Anna Freudian.

In her work at the Hampstead War Nurseries, Anna Freud considered the environmental as well as internal contributions to, and impingements on, infant development. First and foremost was the parent-infant/young child relationship: continuity of care, emotional containment and structure were seen as supporting development. Adult fearful or otherwise dysregulated states of mind, lack of predictability and rupture of love ties were seen as fertile ground for developmental disturbance. This ground knowledge has been elaborated in attachment studies and sometimes subsumed into attachment theory, but has its origins, amongst other sources, in the collated careful daily observations of the children in the War Nurseries (Freud & Burlingham, 1944).

Anna Freud emphasized that assessing a child and establishing a child's progress in meeting the milestones of life should be measured against the age-appropriate, expectable norms of development (Freud, 1965). She moved away from symptoms to their underlying meaning:

> If symptoms are viewed merely as manifest phenomena, dealing with them remains arid so far as analytic interest is concerned. If the clinician is alerted to see opening up behind these the whole range of possible derivations, causations, and developmental affiliations, the field becomes fascinating, and scrutinizing a child's symptomatology becomes a truly analytic task.
>
> (Freud, 1970, p. 184)

In this quotation Anna Freud reiterates her non-linear approach to development; in her view development takes place across different spheres of functioning and one must allow for progressions, pauses, regressions and jumps in development as the personality integrates various maturational and environmental influences (Freud, 1981). Although, again, there may be a risk that this approach makes cultural assumptions about what "normal" development is, the approach is important because it encourages us to always look at a child's difficulties in the context of their overall development. This framework of meaning-making underpins PPIP thinking.

Defences in the adult and the infant

In *Ego and the Mechanisms of Defence* Anna Freud discussed different forms of self-protection adopted by the individual to ward off pain (Freud, 1936). The rich array of defences the book describes characterize the more organized functioning of older children, adolescents and adults. Of particular importance in our work with parents who appear to be intergenerationally repeating aspects of trauma is that of identification with the aggressor. It involves the victim identifying with and adopting the behaviour of a person who is more powerful and hostile towards them in an attempt to master the anxiety and "narcissistic mortification" (Freud, 1936, p. 121) of helplessness and passivity. The parent-infant psychotherapist has to hold in mind both the adult position – that identification with the aggressor is a defence against regressive states in the parent – and the infant's predicament and defence against this aggression.

Infant defences have been mentioned earlier (Chapter 3). To these we add the central defence of inhibition of attachment behaviours. Anna Freud wrote about inhibition that presents as an ego-restriction: a person defends against, for example, painful or shaming external stimuli by abandoning the activity. An infant whose biological inclination is to attract adult protection through his ordinary attachment behaviours of smiling, cooing and calling for his parent's care inhibits these behaviours in the face of parental apathy, rejection or outright hostility. An example is a father who was feeding his 6-month-old baby. He gave the bottle and the infant sucked hungrily. Father then withdrew the bottle saying to the therapist that the baby was no longer hungry. The baby himself had given no indication of satiation but did not protest when the bottle was taken away. Only a while later, when his father gave him the bottle again, did the baby disclose his hunger and deprivation by devouring the bottle. The father's decision to take the bottle away from his baby, while keeping it within the infant's sight, impressed the therapist as teasing him with the bottle's presence but inaccessibility, and signalled to the therapist a possible identification with his own father who had physically abused his sons. The baby's lack of protest suggested he had learned to inhibit his hungry demands, possibly to avoid paternal wrath.

Developmental therapy

Anna Freud moved beyond more traditional models of psychoanalytic therapy, which she thought were most helpful for children who had already achieved a degree of healthy development, and advocated the use for some children of "developmental therapy" (Hurry, 1998), also described as "psychodynamic developmental therapy" (Fonagy & Target, 1996), to address developmental deficits "in which the very building blocks of the personality fail to be properly put in place" (Midgley, 2012, p. 152). When working with developmental therapy, the tools of therapy aim to construct the missing building blocks through, for example, verbalization of feelings when the language for emotions is lacking, or linking cause and effect when external and internal events are experienced as random and meaningless (Edgcumbe, 2000; Fonagy,

Moran, Edgcumbe, Kennedy, & Target, 1993). These are equally relevant in work with parents who display developmental deficits in emotional regulation, mentalization and capacities for symbolization, and with their babies who lack immediate, direct experiences of mental scaffolding from their parents.

The PPIP model in its early years

In its earliest forms, PPIP followed other psychodynamic models of parent-infant psychotherapy and focused primarily on understanding and working through impingements to sensitive mothering (Fraiberg, 1980; Lieberman, Weston, & Pawl, 1991; Marvin, Cooper, Hoffman, & Powell, 2002; Muir, 1992). This conceptualization of the "work" of parent-infant psychotherapy centred on the mind of the mother in relation to her baby: the factors that influenced the specific prism through which she constructed her motherhood and mothering. The psychodynamic hypothesis was organized around the question of what inhibited the occurrence of primary maternal preoccupation and of the mother "claiming" and cherishing her baby (Baradon et al., 2016). This approach drew heavily on the work of the previously mentioned pioneers, and especially Fraiberg, complemented by insights of attachment research into intergenerational transmission of patterns of relating. For example, the Adult Attachment Interview (Hesse, 2016) was routinely conducted with parents to identify their attachment representations and the ways in which the parent's singular narrative of their past may be repeated in the specific present with their infant. This would then be addressed in relation to interactions observed in the session that seemed to impact the baby's feelings of safety and threat. The emphasis was on verbal-representational aspects of therapy – namely reconstruction and interpretation to understand the mother's current psychic functioning in relation to her baby.

Towards a multi-directional model

The rather uni-directional theoretical model (mother to infant) that characterized early parent-infant psychotherapy generally and PPIP specifically in its initial phase was tempered by growing research evidence on infant development. This work opened up a view of the social baby and the bi-directional nature of relationships. Furthermore, the founding PPIP therapists had all been trained in the tradition of infant observation in psychoanalysis and child psychotherapy. In infant observation, a naturalistic observation of earliest development, the trainee learns to follow the nuances of maternal care and the responses and contributions of the baby to the dynamics of their relationship. Indeed, as clinical experience in PPIP grew, the therapists became more adept at observing infant communications and the back and forth of their interactions with their parents in the moment.

Over time, the baby became a more frequent port of entry into the dynamics of the relationship. This shift, conceptually and in practice, to genuinely seeing and hearing the baby "as subject" (Thomson Salo, 2007; Thomson Salo et al., 1999) is fundamental to how PPIP work is currently practised. The baby is equally included in the therapy as a patient in his/her own right, and a substantial element of the thinking in the therapy is baby-led. This means that the adult's material is thought about not only in terms of its meaning for the adult as parent, it also undergoes translation to "how is this experienced and what does this mean for the baby?" For example, a mother is depressed, and the sources and manifestations of her depression are explored with the therapist. At the same time, the therapist observes that the mother responds slowly to her 3-month-old baby's attempts to engage with her. The therapist imagines how the baby, with her unique temperament and in accordance with her age, may experience this time lag in her mother's responses. She will observe the baby's emotional expressions and behaviours – does the baby express herself loudly, perhaps to penetrate the fog of mother's inattention. Is the baby's body tone slumping, her expectation of responsivity diminished? Perhaps she is becoming withdrawn and blank in anxious retreat. The therapist's activity of *imagining the infant's embodied feelings* and emerging visceral-representational world has a double function. It gives voice, shape and agency to the baby himself or herself, and it helps the parent acknowledge the real baby before him/her, the partner in their relationship.

The therapeutic model has also been extended through inclusion of fathers/others as active partners. This added layer of father/third/triad changed PPIP from a mother-infant to a parent/parents-infant therapy in a very genuine way. On the one hand, as mentioned in Chapter 2, there is the real-life "father-third" for the infant, and on the other hand, there is the father/progenitor. Even when the father is not physically present in the family's life and/or in therapy room, he will be present in the therapist's mind as progenitor, partner (or not) and as father. Bringing the fathers/others in, so to speak, also opened the door to thinking about the familial, cultural and professional networks around and in interaction (or not) with the family.

And, last but not least, the PPIP model and its practice also gives careful thought to the influences of the therapist on the interactions in the room and the clinical process: this is the focus of ongoing microanalytic research at the AFC into clinical process (for more on this see Chapter 7). The inclusion of the therapist-as-participant brings a wider systemic dimension into the consulting room. In a research project using frame-by-frame analysis to study the interactions between all participants, the researchers concluded that interactions do not move between dyads, so much as seem to move as a spiral between all participants over time, and it is often difficult to trace the "beginning" of the transactional chain (Avdi et al., 2020).

Embodied communication

The focus on the experience and communications of the baby brought about a significant change in the "languages" used for communication in PPIP. Whereas focus on the parent's mind privileges verbal discourse, increasing attention to the baby-as-patient shifted attention to the embodied domain in the processes of communication and meaning-making. PPIP therapists are now highly sensitized to emotional undertones conveyed audially (tone, pitch, vocal rhythm), through visual cues (facial expression, gaze), movement (gesture, posture and body orientation) and time (pauses, silences, turn taking). This sits with trauma-informed therapy for adults, which has also shifted focus to the body and embodied communications (van der Kolk, 2014).

Verbal and non-verbal communication are in dynamic interaction. In attuned communications between therapist, parent and baby, verbal and embodied languages reinforce the affective meaning of the other. Bodily communication non-consciously scaffolds the verbal communication and verbal communication amplifies/clarifies the embodied message. For the baby, someone putting their experience into words provides them with the label (concept) with which to recognize emotion as well as introducing the early rhythms of language. Moving between these modes of communication gives the sessions a musicality that characterizes sharing of states with the actual baby and the emotional states of the adult/s. Furthermore, the relationship between verbal and embodied discourse and the weave and discordance between the different forms of communication, both between parent and infant (Beebe, Lachmann, Markese, & Bahrick, 2012) and between the dyad or triad and therapist, have become central sources for understanding the clinical process (Avdi & Seikkula, 2019; Baradon, 2018).

Transference and countertransference

The repetition of significant aspects of earliest attachment relationships in present personal relationships plays a key role in any psychological treatment. In parents "the raw emotions of their earliest relationships with their parents (i.e., the baby's grandparents) are often expressed in their relationship with their baby" (Baradon et al., 2016). Therefore, whereas in many analytically based therapies the transference to the therapist is the main instrument of the therapy, in PPIP therapy it is the parent's/parents' transference to the baby that is usually the avenue of work. The aim is to relieve the baby of impingements on their development that result from the force of parental transference. However, this position does not diminish the importance of understanding the parent's transference to the therapist – whether or not it is worked with directly.

A positive transference may make it easier for a parent to identify with the therapist's compassion for his/her wounded infantile self and, thereby, also towards his or her baby. It suggests that there are nurturing and protective figures in the parent's internal world who can be allies to this work. However, as discussed, many of the parents in PPIP bring a traumatic attachment history which infiltrates the relationship with the therapist through negative and/or fraught transference, which may need to be addressed directly. If, for example, the parent is no longer taking in interventions and does not find them helpful, we may wonder whether there has been a breakdown in trust in the therapeutic relationship, and the patient has become closed to the therapist's emotional and social communications. The therapist may be alerted to triggers of negativity in the parent's relationship with their infant that mirror the parent transference to the therapist (e.g., a parent who finds the baby's gaze intrusive may be alluding to their experience of the therapist). In addition, transference indications can inform the therapist about the parent's habitual maladaptive ways-of-being-with attachment figures and how this may cause "social thinning" (see Chapter 2) of their social support system (many PPIP patients are socially isolated and this is an important risk factor in the perinatal period).

An interesting discussion is taking place about whether babies, too, may manifest negative transference behaviours, as when a baby displays anxious avoidance towards the therapist (e.g., Salomonsson & Sandell, 2011). In this context, we understand transference manifestation in terms of what the baby is telling us about the emotional valence of formative experiences with his or her parent/parents. Transference behaviours in a baby need to be distinguished from situations where the baby is the mouthpiece for the parent. For example,

> A ten-month old refused to enter the consulting room. Hanging on to his mother's hand to support his walking, he stalled at the doorway. Mother looked at the therapist with a helpless expression. The same behaviour occurred the following session. The therapist was puzzled: her attempts to engage him through play and to address the baby and mother in terms of his possible displeasures were not particularly successful. What also registered was a triumphant undertone

to mother's "what can I do if he doesn't like you" smile. The therapist wondered about mother's ambivalence being expressed via the
baby. The baby's reluctance disappeared when mother was helped to
express her anger with the therapist and they could reflect on this.

Countertransference refers to the largely unconscious feelings and
thoughts evoked in the therapist by her experience of being with the
patient/s. Not surprisingly, the baby's presence in the room can evoke
strong countertransference feelings in the therapist, such as a wish to
rescue a vulnerable infant or the opposite – feelings of disgust at a really
snotty nose or smelly nappy, or at the evacuative processes they represent. Parents' struggles too can be emotionally arousing. It is common for
trainee practitioners to be highly critical of the parent/parents, evidencing the successful tug of infants at the adult's attachment heartstrings. Or
the therapist may feel motherly or fatherly compassion for a parent who
is her- or himself flooded by unmet infantile needs.

Trauma and PPIP

Trauma is increasingly a central focus of PPIP. In this context, the spotlight is on identifying what constitutes the trauma in the parent-infant
interactions and how quickly and appropriately transactions that dysregu-
late the baby are recognized and addressed and interactive repair takes
place (Tronick & Gianino, 1986). There are various embodied channels
that inform the parent-infant psychotherapist of relational trauma in the
consulting room.

We have mentioned parental behaviours that are known to be associated with disorganized outcomes in the baby as well as the direct
communications by the baby about his experience. These include facial
expression, cry and other distressed vocalizations, orientation and the
baby's use of defences which distort normative, expectable behaviours
(in Chapter 3).

Another source of information regarding trauma are the back- and-
forth interactions between parent and infant as they co-construct their
singular dance. The occurrence of the "unexpected" may signal to the
therapist that trauma has infiltrated the ongoing caretaking transactions.
An illustration of such dyadic construction occurred in interactions
between a mother and baby in which the mother responded to a young
baby's crying with apparently appropriate attempts at soothing, but
which were met with increasing upset. The baby, surprisingly, stopped
crying only when put down on the floor. This counter-intuitive
sequence suggested that the mother's agitation and anger were conveyed

to the baby through bodily contact (e.g., when holding the baby against her chest and rocking), and the floor provided a safer holding environment at that point.

Last but far from least is the information gleaned from the therapist's own attachment and countertransference systems. The therapist's response can also inform us about the experience of the other. For example, the following sessional notes describe the response of a therapist to a sudden unusual behaviour of a mother:

> Not only did it take me completely by surprise, but I felt disrupted in my own experience of going-on-being, and my shared experience with the baby. . . . The impact was highly dysregulating of my affective state and disorganising of my thought processes.
>
> (Baradon, 2018)

Such strong feelings in the therapist may explain how traumatizing the mother's behaviours were for the baby and why she, aged 4 months, relied so heavily on global avoidance and withdrawal (this case is described in Chapter 6).

Working with strengths

The perinatal period is seen as a window of opportunity for intervention. An infant's developmental push and hardwiring for attachment and a parent's reparative wishes to do the best for their child are a powerful combination and potential drivers for change.

In PPIP it is as important for the therapist to work with the dyad's or triad's strengths as with the disturbance in their relationship. Parents often come to the therapy heavily burdened with a sense of failure and shame as parents and full of guilt towards their baby. These feelings may get in the way of recognizing both their positive contributions to their baby's wellbeing and, importantly, the baby's positive moves towards them. At a very simple level, sometimes pointing out a baby's (unnoticed) "special smile for mummy" can be as helpful as reflecting on a parent's feelings of rejection or worthlessness. Babies are also very responsive to changes in the parent's response. An infant who fails to attract his or her parent's/parents' live attention may eventually withdraw, as shown also in the Still Face experiments (Tronick, Als, Adamson, Wise, & Brazelton, 1978; Weinberg & Tronick, 1996). However, when a parent begins to respond, the baby's initiatives are rewarded and will trigger more initiative in the baby and, thus, more rewards for the parent.

Lieberman and colleagues have argued for the importance of uncovering past angels in traumatized nurseries – those early benevolent emotional experiences with primary love objects that bestow upon the baby a sense of having been protected and cared for. These may be memories of a particular figure, such as grandparent or neighbour, or feeling states of safety at particular times that have endowed the parent with some ability to trust another (Lieberman, Padrón, Van Horn, & Harris, 2005). With trauma dramatically in the foreground, such figures may remain elusive or far from conscious feelings of wellbeing. Intentional enquiry about positive attachment experiences and elaboration of them can bring them alive in the parent's mind. The authors say that

> uncovering angels as growth p-romoting forces in the lives of traumatized parents is as vital to the work of psychotherapy as is the interpretation and exorcizing of ghost. . . . [we see] the reemergence of these benevolent figures in consciousness as an instrument of therapeutic change.
>
> (p. 504)

One of the objectives of PPIP is to generate an embodied resonance between past feelings of trust in helpful figures and aspects of the therapeutic relationship which may form the basis for the therapeutic alliance and the challenging work of change. Furthermore, a parent who is conscious of, and emotionally in touch with, experiences of being loved and cared for may find it easier to be temperate in responding to the vulnerabilities and dependency of their infant. Times where the parent is asked to respond to their child in ways that they were not parented may be more tolerable when memories of benign adults – albeit not necessarily their parents – are accessible. This is particularly true in child protection cases, when the parent has to accept the involvement of social services and the courts with them and their children but were failed by those very agencies in their own childhood.

The therapist as a new object

Another aspect of strengths lies in the use the parents and baby make of the therapist. As we know, psychological reorganization during the perinatal period offers a real window of opportunity for new and transformative experiences. For example, Stern proposes that a new mother will, from pregnancy, start forming a "maternal matrix" – a "unique self-system" organized around the care for her child (Stern, 1995). Where the new mother lacks a benign representation of her mother from her own childhood, "the mother's engagement in the therapeutic relationship provides her with several other possible mothers that she could realistically be or become and with several other mothers she could stop being or avoid becoming" (Stern, 1995, p. 112). In other words, the procedural experiences with the therapist as a concerned and nurturing object may support the internalization of a supportive transgenerational motherhood constellation: a benign maternal grandmother, whose presence as an internal object the mother can access and pass on to the infant. The first author of this book, Baradon, has suggested that experiences of the therapist's care can enable the creation of angels within the therapeutic situation. "An emergent procedural angel", she writes, can develop through her or his "interest, compassion, reflectiveness towards the traumatised infant in the parent . . . and her receptivity and pleasure towards the baby" (Baradon, 2009, p. 209–210). This links to literature on the patient's discovery of the analyst as a "new object" (Baker, 1993). Baker suggests that the analyst fosters new object experiences through verbal interpretation of transference distortions and non-verbal provision of experiences of "safety and tolerance" (Baker, 1993, p. 1) that negate negative transference expectations. To this we would add other positions the therapist may take that reinforce "new object" experiences and diminish transferential mistrust. One aspect of this is linked to the idea of "developmental help" advocated by Anna Freud, which has also informed mentalization theory, such as the therapist makes their thinking transparent ("I said this to you because I noticed that . . ."). This anchors the therapist's thinking in shared experience in the room and establishes sharing and thinking as safe and meaningful rather than inexplicable and persecutory.

The therapist as new object for the baby

For many baby patients, the relationship with the PPIP therapist may hold an important key to development, especially when their parent/parents are unable to respond to infantile states of dependency and urgency, and there is very little pleasure in their relationship, or even hostility. The PPIP therapist through, for example, noticing the baby's communications, wanting to understand their meaning, and enjoying interactions with baby, may be instrumental in keeping alive normal attachment-seeking behaviours when they are in danger of closing down into a withdrawn, depressed state. It is important to emphasize that the therapist's importance to the baby is normally transient and as the parent recovers nurturing capacities the baby will turn to the parent over the therapist.

Fathers and the nuclear family

As mentioned, in the past decade or so there has been a significant move in the PPIP model to include fathers whenever they play a role in the baby's life. This may entail father's participation in the entire course of therapy, or when he can, or just a few times. The father may attend in order to help his partner whose state of mind is disturbed in her recent motherhood and/or to support a troubled mother-baby relationship, or out of the wish to better parent his infant, with an awareness that his own conflicts and unresolved issues are interfering with this (Baradon, 2019a). Thus, the depth of work with the father may range from working with mother and baby "in the presence of" the father to directly addressing his experience of becoming a father, his mental health and his relationship with his infant. The role the father chooses to play within the therapy, and the use he chooses to make of it, depends not only on his personal and cultural inclinations, but also on the mother's willingness to share the therapeutic space with him and on both parent's capacities' for triadification (see Chapter 2). In addition, (often unconscious) factors in the therapist influence the extent and quality of a father's participation; for example, his or her own experiences with fathers and men, ease at working within a family group in which s/he is both an insider and outsider, how comfortable s/he feels working with the couple's sexuality (Baradon, 2019b; Segal, 2019).

The father's participation in the session enables the therapeutic work to encompass the patterns of nurturance between the adults and their support for each other's relationship with their baby, experiences in becoming a family and issues of triangulation. As noted by Belsky, the parents can work towards splitting and exclusion or towards "a truly interactive triad in which positive marital communication and stimulating, positive and responsive mothering and fathering can occur" (Belsky & Volling, 1987, p. 54). The therapist would attend to whether the baby has the experience of a parental couple that works together to hold him, or is he pulled into alliances with one parent at the expense of a fluid relationship with the other parent and the upholding of generational boundaries. These are critical to the sense of safety and creativity of each member and the family system.

Race, religion and culture

Race, religion and culture have been in the background of PPIP from its inception, since waves of migration have been reflected in the clinical population referred for therapy. However, discussion within a session of the meaning of race, religion and culture in a direct way is relatively recent. A PPIP therapist reported that some years ago she treated a baby, mother and mother's mother – the baby's maternal grandmother to whom guardianship had been transferred by the Courts due to the young mother's depression and neglect of her child. These three generations of Afro-Caribbean women had a personal history of uprootedness, poverty and violence; by contrast, the therapist was white, middle-class English born. The therapist noted, in retrospect, how the differences between them and their possible significance to the family were not mentioned throughout the work together. Nor were they thought about much by her or raised in supervision. She contemplated the possible significance of broader systemic aspects of this family's life – racial, economic, educational, power, relationships with the state authorities, etc. – and what may have been missed through lack of exploration of this. Despite this, a working alliance was formed between the three generations in the family and the therapist, which brought positive changes in parenting of the baby. But, she wondered: could the therapy be considered "real-enough" and were the relationships in the room authentic enough for the therapy to be seen as completed?

What we know now to have been excluded from this therapy are swathes of experience, emotions and representation regarding fundamental issues of identity. Indeed, it is now recognized that "Theorizing gender and sexuality, race and class, cultural difference and religious or spiritual values in the psychoanalytic space is no longer seen as an 'extra' set of variables to be taken into account, but as fundamental to the dialogue with the unconscious" (Smith, 2013).

"What I have learned", said the therapist, "is that, in my eagerness to reach out to this grandmother, mother and baby, I at some level chose to be blind to otherness rather than acknowledging and reflecting on it. Perhaps I was not very different to many other therapists at that time, but can you imagine the contorted manoeuvring we – the disempowered women in the family and I, guilty in my privilege – had to do to in order to reach each other?" This therapist's personal account reflects the view, held also by the authors, that being able to engage constructively with such aspects of identity as relational variables relies on the individual's ability to acknowledge their own racial, gendered, class and power-related identity and the constructs that influenced the formation of that singular identity. This awareness is essential to the capacity to reflect about the impact of "who I am" on the other, including on the baby, and on the therapeutic relationship.

The professional network

Contrary to the tradition of psychoanalysis, parent-infant psychotherapy has always seen itself as part of the professional network. The vulnerability of the baby and the possibility of conflict between the best interests of the baby and those of the parent always require an ongoing working relationship with other professionals involved with the family. Indeed, when there is not a functioning network and concerns about safety and wellbeing of either baby or parent/parents arise, it may be the PPIP therapist who initiates putting a network in place as a team around the family. The question of confidentiality always arises for both family and therapist in the context of network communication. The process would follow usual safe-guarding best practice: confidentiality would be maintained regarding therapeutic process as far as assessment of risk allows. Furthermore, communication with the network is shared with and transparent to the family, unless counter-indicated.

> For example, a couple with severe mental health and addiction histories had a 4-month-old baby for whom they were caring well with input from a variety of agencies. The father was receiving mentalization based therapy for BPD, the mother was in an Alcoholics Anonymous support group and her General Practitioner and the local Children Centre were also supporting her and the baby, and the family were receiving weekly PPIP sessions. Amongst the many professionals, it was only the PPIP therapist who had a picture of the whole family and the interplay of individual and couple dynamics on the baby and each other. When a crisis arose in the father's life, there was a collapse of mother's mental health and the couple's ability to meet the needs of the baby. However, the connection between father's and mother's health was not picked up by the agencies who worked with each parent separately. Moreover, the agencies were focused on the adults whereas the PPIP therapist held the anxiety of "what will happen to baby if both parents become ill again?" The PPIP therapist instigated a network meeting with all the professionals and the parents to bring together the separate and isolated strands. Issues of confidentiality were discussed with the parents ahead of the meeting in terms of what information they felt comfortable to share in the broader forum. There was also exploration of the common phantasy that the agencies would want to remove their baby. In the meeting the confidential relationship between professional and client was maintained and the familial predicament was thought about; this significantly improved the support the network was able to offer and the family to accept.

What this illustration highlights is the need for a systemic view of the family when most services are focused on supporting the individual parent, the need also to talk to the family about their fears and hopes from a coordinated network, and that confidentiality and respect for the therapeutic work with individuals within the family can still be held.

However, the functioning of the network may be challenged when it comes to issues of risk to the wellbeing of the infant. Agencies often apply different criteria to what constitutes risk and what levels of risk require more formal intervention, especially in relation to emotional abuse. This is a familiar scenario when resources are limited and, for example, social services accept only cases at highest end of risk. Difficulties within the professional network can also emerge when different professionals identify with different members of the family (Trowell & Bowe, 1995), with the result sometimes that the baby is lost from view. Keeping the baby alive in the network's mind and actively representing the baby's developmental needs and timetable may be particular contributions of the PPIP therapist. In the experience of the clinicians at the AFC, the expertise of the therapist as the voice of the baby within the professional discussion is usually highly valued and can significantly influence processes and outcomes for the baby.

Assessing risk

In the course of the therapy, therapists are required at times to manage high levels of anxiety in themselves and in the network regarding the wellbeing of the baby in the care of their parents.

A number of factors place further pressure on the assessment of risk in infancy.

- Working under pressure of the baby's developmental timetable. It is somewhat of a mantra in the infant mental health field that "babies can't wait". By this it is meant that windows of opportunity for environmental input to development open up at certain times, and are missed to the detriment of the child's development. Therefore, interventions to support environmental nurturance have a clock ticking away. But entrenched pathology in the parent may not shift at pace: time may be needed to build trust, to establish shared goals for the therapy that focus on the baby and parent's development, to apprehend changes needed and to develop different procedures of being-with-the-other. The parent's capacity to do this psychological work may be impeded by personality structures as well as defences. The therapist has to assess whether the changes that are taking place are sufficient and rapid enough to meet the baby's developmental timetable in the broadest sense.
- In the course of the sessions a relationship will have formed with the parent, often a meaningful one. The relationship can be the basis for discussing concerns in a constructive way, but may also make it more difficult to challenge the parent on risk to the infant: for example, it

can feel cruel to confront the parent with a repetition he or she has so wanted to avoid. The therapist may also be aware that the parent had not been protected as a child, and the parent is being asked to accept that something is being given to the child that the parent did not receive as a child. Sadness and guilt towards the infant in the parent may make it harder to prioritize the present child.

- At times, professional networks can also bring their own challenges. Values and goals may not be shared between the professionals or organizations, responsibilities may be unfairly loaded, certain families act to split the network – eliciting contradictory identifications (e.g., with mother vs with child) that introduce conflict between professionals. Thus, working within a network may add to stress, particularly when the response to a therapist raising concerns about a baby is dismissive ("the health visitor is not worried", "the psychiatrist says mum is doing fine"). Issues such as limited resources, high thresholds for referral, interorganizational relations, personalities of the practitioners all play a role. We hypothesize that, in addition, defences against the suffering of the baby may make it difficult for the therapist to effectively represent an overlooked baby. Yet it is his or her expertise in imagining the internal world of the baby that makes the therapist so well equipped to be their "voice".

References

Avdi, E., Amiran, K., Baradon, T., Broughton, C., Sleed, M., Spencer, R., & Shai, D. (2020). Studying the process of psychoanalytic parent-infant psychotherapy: Embodied and discursive aspects. *Infant Mental Health Journal*, *41*(5), 589–602. doi:10.1002/imhj.21888

Avdi, E., & Seikkula, J. (2019). Studying the process of psychoanalytic psychotherapy: Discursive and embodied aspects. *British Journal of Psychotherapy*, *35*(2), 217–232. doi:10.1111/bjp.12444

Baker, R. (1993). The patient's discovery of the psychoanalyst as a new object. *International Journal of Psycho-Analysis*, *74*(6), 1223–1233.

Baradon, T. (2009). *Relational trauma in infancy: Psychoanalytic, attachment and neuropsychological contributions to parent–infant psychotherapy*. Abingdon: Routledge.

Baradon, T. (2018). Microanalysis of multimodal communication in therapy: A case of relational trauma in parent-infant psychoanalytic psychotherapy. *Journal of Infant, Child, and Adolescent Psychotherapy*, *17*(1), 1–13. doi:10.1080/15289168.2017.1415101

Baradon, T. (2019a). *Working with fathers in psychoanalytic parent-infant psychotherapy*. London: Routledge.

Baradon, T. (2019b). Working with the triad. In *Working with fathers in psychoanalytic parent-infant psychotherapy*. London: Routledge.

Baradon, T., Biseo, M., Broughton, C., James, J., & Joyce, A. (2016). *The practice of psychoanalytic parent-infant psychotherapy: Claiming the baby* (2nd ed.). London: Routledge.

Baradon, T., & Broughton, C. (2005). *The practice of psychoanalytic parent-infant psychotherapy: Claiming the baby*. London: Routledge.

Barlow, J., Bennett, C., Midgley, N., Larkin, S. K., & Wei, Y. (2015). Parent-infant psychotherapy for improving parental and infant mental health. *Cochrane Database of Systematic Reviews, 1*(1), Cd010534. doi:10.1002/14651858.CD010534.pub2

Beebe, B., Lachmann, F., Markese, S., & Bahrick, L. (2012). On the origins of disorganized attachment and internal working models: Paper I. A dyadic systems approach. *Psychoanalytic Dialogues, 22*(2), 253–272. doi:10.1080/10481885.2012.666147

Belsky, J., & Volling, B. L. (1987). Mothering, fathering, and marital interaction in the family triad during infancy: Exploring family system's processes. In P. W. Berman & F. A. Pederson (Eds.), *Men's transitions to parenthood: Longitudinal studies of early family experience* (pp. 37–63). New York: Psychology Press.

Cramer, B. (1999) *Parents et enfants: Bertrand Cramer, quel bilan tirez-vous de votre carrière de bébologue?/Interviewer: A. Racine*. France: Le Temps.

Edgcumbe, R. (2000). *Anna Freud: A view of development, disturbance and therapeutic techniques*. London: Routledge.

Fonagy, P., Moran, G. S., Edgcumbe, R., Kennedy, H., & Target, M. (1993). The roles of mental representations and mental processes in therapeutic action. *Psychoanalytic Study of the Child, 48*, 9–48. doi:10.1080/00797308.1993.11822377

Fonagy, P., & Target, M. (1996). A contemporary psychoanalytic perspective: Psychodynamic developmental therapy. In E. D. Hibbs & P. S. Jensen (Eds.), *Psychosocial treatments for child and adolescent disorders: Empirically based strategies for clinical practice* (pp. 619–638). Washington, DC: National Institutes of Health and American Psychological Association.

Fraiberg, S. (1980). *Clinical studies in infant mental health: The first year of life*. New York, NY: Basic Books.

Freud, A. (1936). *The ego and the mechanisms of defence*. New York, NY: International Universities Press, 1946.

Freud, A. (1965). *Normality and pathology in childhood: Assessments of development*. Madison, CT: International Universities Press.

Freud, A. (1970). The symptomatology of childhood: A preliminary classification. *The Psychoanalytic Study of the Child, 25*(1), 19–41.

Freud, A. (1981). The concept of developmental lines: Their diagnostic significance. *Psychoanalytic Study of the Child, 36*, 129–136.

Freud, A., & Burlingham, D. (1944). Infants without families: Reports on the Hampstead Nurseries. In *The writings of Anna Freud* (Vol. 3). New York, NY: International Universities Press.

Goldstein, J. (1982). Anna Freud. *The Yale Law Journal, 92*(2), 219–227.

Hesse, E. (2016). The adult attachment interview: Protocol, method of analysis, and empirical studies. In J. Cassidy & P. R. Shaver (Eds.), *Handbook of attachment: Theory, research, and clinical applications* (4th ed., pp. 553–597). New York, NY: Guilford Press.

Hurry, A. (1998). Psychoanalysis and developmental therapy. In A. Hurry (Ed.), *Psychoanalysis and developmental theory* (pp. 32–73). London: Karnac.

Lieberman, A. F., Padrón, E., Van Horn, P., & Harris, W. W. (2005). Angels in the nursery: The intergenerational transmission of benevolent parental influences. *Infant Mental Health Journal*, *26*(6), 504–520. doi:doi:10.1002/imhj.20071

Lieberman, A. F., Weston, D. R., & Pawl, J. H. (1991). Preventive intervention and outcome with anxiously attached dyads. *Child Development*, *62*(1), 199–209.

Marvin, R., Cooper, G., Hoffman, K., & Powell, B. (2002). The circle of security project: Attachment-based intervention with caregiver-pre-school child dyads. *Attachment and Human Development*, *4*, 107–124.

Midgley, N. (2007). Anna Freud: The Hampstead war nurseries and the role of the direct observation of children for psychoanalysis. *International Journal of Psycho-Analysis*, *88*(4), 939–959. doi:10.1516/V28R-J334-6182-524H

Midgley, N. (2012). *Reading Anna Freud*. London: Routledge.

Muir, E. (1992). Watching, waiting, and wondering: Applying psychoanalytic principles to mother-infant intervention. *Infant Mental Health Journal*, *13*(4), 319–328. doi:10.1002/1097–0355(199224)13:4<319::Aid-Imhj2280130407>3.0.Co;2–2

Salomonsson, B., & Sandell, R. (2011). A randomized controlled trial of mother–infant psychoanalytic treatment: I. Outcomes on self-report questionnaires and external ratings. *Infant Mental Health Journal*, *32*(2), 207–231. doi:10.1002/imhj.20291

Segal, Y. (2019). The therapist and the father in parent-infant psychotherapy. In *Working with fathers in psychoanalytic parent-infant psychotherapy*. London: Routledge.

Smith, C. (2013). Naming and otherness: South African intersubjective psychoanalytic psychotherapy and the negotiation of racialised histories. In M. O'Loughlin, G. Lobban, & C. Smith (Eds.), *Psychodynamic psychotherapy in South Africa: Contexts, theories and applications* (pp. 13–30). Johannesburg: Wits University Press.

Solis-Ponton, L. (2001). Sur la notion de parentalité développée par Serge Lebovici. *Spirale*, *1*(17), 135–141.

Stern, D. N. (1995). *The motherhood constellation: A unified view of parent-infant psycho-therapy*. New York: Basic Books.

Tauzin, T., & Gergely, G. (2019). Variability of signal sequences in turn-taking exchanges induces agency attribution in 10.5-mo-olds. *Proceedings of the National Academy of Sciences of the United States of America*, *116*(31), 15441–15446. doi:10.1073/pnas.1816709116

Thomson Salo, F. (2007). Recognizing the infant as subject in infant-parent psychotherapy. *The International Journal of Psychoanalysis*, *88*(4), 961–979. doi:10.1516/D67X-384K-9888-210J

Thomson Salo, F., Paul, C., Morgan, A., Jones, S., Jordan, B., Meehan, M., . . . Walker, A. (1999). "Free to be playful": Therapeutic work with infants. *Infant Observation*, *3*(1), 47–62. doi:10.1080/13698039908400854

Tronick, E., Als, H., Adamson, L., Wise, S., & Brazelton, T. B. (1978). The infant's response to entrapment between contradictory messages in face-to-face interaction. *Journal of the American Academy of Child and Adolescent Psychiatry*, *17*(1), 1–13.

Tronick, E., & Gianino, A. (1986). The transmission of maternal disturbance to the infant. In E. Tronick & T. Field (Eds.), *Maternal depression and infant disturbance* (pp. 5–11). San Francisco, CA: Jossey-Bass.

Trowell, J., & Bowe, M. (1995). *The emotional needs of children and young families*. London: Routledge.

van der Kolk, B. (2014). *The body keeps the score: Mind, brain and body in the transformation of trauma*. London: Penguin.

Weinberg, K. M., & Tronick, E. Z. (1996). Infant affective reactions to the resumption of maternal interaction after the still-face. *Child Development, 67*, 905–914.

5   Mentalizing and infancy

In this chapter we will think about the relationship between mentalizing and infancy. As mentioned in Chapter 1, mentalizing is defined as the social cognitive process by which we imagine and try to understand both our ourselves and other people in terms of their underlying mental states – feelings, thoughts, beliefs, ideas and knowledge. One of the motivations for writing this book comes from the idea that the existing literature on mentalization-based treatments (MBT) has tended to focus on early relational experiences in terms of their developmental consequences in children, adolescents and adults. MBT was originally developed in the 1990s as an intervention for adults with borderline personality disorder. It has since been adapted and developed for use for many different treatment groups and settings and is now used to treat a range of diagnoses, such as depression, eating disorders and psychosis, as well as other forms of personality disorder. It has been modified for children and adolescents, as well as parents and foster-parents (for an overview, see Bateman & Fonagy, 2019). But here we would like to explore further the mentalizing experiences of parents and infants while in the midst of babyhood and its demands; we believe this may anchor thinking about the earliest stage of life more distinctively in mentalizing theory, and may suggest routes for the further clinical development of both PPIP and MBT-informed practice.

We will begin with the baby and their mentalizing needs: in early infancy, the driver for all experience and selfhood is affect – feeling states – and the baby is not able to differentiate whether the source of pleasure or unpleasure is internal or external. Parental care provides the concepts that will come to label and make sense of the affect, which forms the cornerstone of thinking about experience and ultimately generates a coherent sense of self, as discussed in Introduction. This explains why it is important to understand the different ways in which parents can helpfully or unhelpfully understand the mental states of their baby. An infant whose parent is significantly (e.g., through hostile misattributions) and consistently unable

DOI: 10.4324/9781003024323-5

to recognize, understand and mirror back to them something of what they are experiencing is at risk of not only having their immediate needs unmet, they are also missing out on a process that scaffolds early development. From a now fairly wide body of research, we have extensive and valuable accounts of how the experience of being inadequately mentalized in the early years may affect the individual's own nascent capacity to mentalize, as well as their attachment status, their capacity for self-regulation and their socio-emotional development more generally (for a comprehensive review see Luyten, Campbell, Allison, & Fonagy, 2020).

When we discuss parental mentalizing, we do not only mean their verbal expressions or particularly reflective, conscious thoughts about what is going on for their baby. In infancy, much of the baby's experience is embodied, as is the parent's response. Researchers of embodied experience, Fotopoulou and Tsakiris, have powerfully argued that the most basic elements of our sense of self are shaped by our embodied interactions with others: "the very first-person experience of my body as mine, as well as the building block of the self-other distinction, are constituted upon the presence of other bodies in proximity and interaction" (Fotopoulou & Tsakiris, 2017, p. 13). Because of this saliency of physical interactions in infancy, in this chapter we address embodied mentalizing as well as the verbal domains of mentalizing discussed in MBT literature and treatment guides.

Mentalizing infants, in the issues it raises, seems to us to be different to mentalizing older children. It is often embodied in nature and has a quality of urgency (reflecting the intensity of infant's emotional experience), and it can also sometimes be quite difficult to do – babies often do not know quite what they are experiencing, much less are they able to explain it. In addition, mentalizing is an interpersonal and interactive process: mentalizing is maintained with the help of other minds. It is often emphasized in the MBT literature that it is hard for anyone to hold onto their capacity to think about emotional states in a balanced or robust way when they are operating in a non-mentalizing social environment and/or when emotions are heightened, particularly emotions that trigger the attachment system. While many parents in most circumstances recognize the intentional and personalized nature of their baby's communications, the problem for parents is that a baby is naturally a very arousing attachment agent, bringing powerful raw emotions which can trigger non-mentalizing responses. To compound this, the baby cannot act as the restorative mentalizing other for the parent. For vulnerable parents, and probably for all parents when feeling particularly vulnerable, a young infant may be experienced as the ultimate non-mentalizing social environment – when the parent is besieged by dysregulated affect *and* there is no one to introduce a mentalizing perspective to help bring their own capacity to think back online. Further, mentalizing is associated with self-regulation since in order to adjust and regulate our own behaviour, we need to be cognisant of the mental state underpinning it. When a parent is in aroused state and cannot think coherently, they are not only less able to soothe their baby but may also, in their dysregulated state, become more arousing for the baby and find themselves unable to break the cycle of negative interactions.

There are two ways of approaching mentalizing that are relevant to PPIP: Fonagy and colleagues' cognitive model of mentalizing, and Shai and Belsky's model of embodied mentalizing. Both approaches are based on the assumption of the centrality of the role of thinking about mental states, both in oneself and others. Whereas Fonagy and colleagues' work has focussed on the semantic and declarative expressions of mentalizing, Shai's work on parental embodied mentalizing (PEM) is closer to "the infant's realm of experience, that of quality of movement, rhythms, space, time, sensations and touch" (Shai & Belsky, 2011, p. 187). Basic concepts of mentalizing are described in the following sections.

Effective mentalizing

Good enough, sensitive parenting implies that the parent is able to notice and give meaning to the baby's states, and therefore respond appropriately and contingently. The mother or father (or grandparents, parents, or siblings) in their day-to-day actions are performing an active task: they are making sense of the infant's experience, for the infant. It is out of these exchanges that the building blocks for a sense of self are made – "this is me, this is how I feel, and this is how others understand me to feel". A central concept in this process is marked mirroring, which describes how the parent communicates to the child that they understand what the child is feeling, and that the feeling belongs to the child and the parent can empathize with it.

> For example, when the baby cries that mother looks sad and concerned – frowning, enquiring look, mouth slightly pulled down. "Oh" she says, "What's up sweetheart?" She leans closer to the baby, her head inclined to the side: "It's ok, ah, its ok" and she gives a little encouraging smile.

The complexity of marked mirroring is that the parent is engaging authentically with the child's feelings, while understanding that the feeling belongs to child and showing these feelings are manageable for the parent ("*It's ok, ah, its ok*") (Fonagy, Gergely, Jurist, & Target, 2002). A parent who identifies too strongly with the baby and experiences the baby's feeling as strongly as the baby does will not be able to convey to the baby that the feelings belong to the baby and can be understood and tolerated by the parent. The capacity to express sympathetic understanding of the mental state of the infant as a separate person is a subtle act, but one mastered intuitively by many parents – usually indicating that they themselves have had solid experiences of being mentalized. However, there are certain patterns of parental mentalizing that can impinge on the baby's experience of their own and others' mental states, and disrupt the latent potentiality for robust mentalizing.

Inadequate mentalizing: the non-mentalizing modes

One of the central difficulties parents can bring to how they relate to the infants – from a mentalizing perspective – is a non-mentalizing mode of function, by which we mean one of the following.

Psychic equivalent mode is often characterized in young children by a powerful certainty that what is inside the mind is the same as outside reality – we are familiar with the toddler, for whom the monster in his mind lives in the wardrobe. In a parent, psychic equivalence manifests, for example, in an inability to differentiate between the content of the parent's mind and that of the infant. In such cases the baby may be seen as an extension of themselves – he feels just as I do. Or the parent may attribute to the baby their own state of mind: A parent who is in a bad mood and feeling fed up with their baby and their baby's demands – as all parents inevitably do at times – might, if in a state of psychic equivalence, assume that it is the baby who is angry and hostile (in psychoanalytic terms this would be described as a projection). This can play out in various ways, but makes a potentially negative cycle of interaction between parent and infant more likely, and one in which the infant's actual needs and state are not recognized. Another example would be a parent who is feeling frightened or threatened and comes to assume there is a real threat to their child.

Pretend mode is another form of non-mentalizing, initially described by Fonagy and Target in their work on "playing with reality" (Fonagy & Target, 1996). In this mode, the boundaries between reality and fantasy are blurred and perspective-taking is difficult. A parent caught up in pretend mode may construct a theory about the child's behaviour, for example, "my (3-month-old) baby's doing this to me to wind me up, she's so determined and knows exactly how to upset me" – without referencing a reality, such as the child's age (in this case 3 months), which may challenge their conviction that the child can knowingly and intentionally plan to wind them up.

The third non-mentalizing mode is *teleological mode*. This describes the way in which a person may rely on concrete actions or cues about emotional states in order to recognize them as valid or real. Teleological mode in infants is expressed in their need for physical reassurance and their very embodied relationship with the world and others. Adults operating in teleological mode may demand physical or visual proof of mental states – that is, "My baby's not crying, therefore she can't be sad, therefore she is fine". Such a concrete mode of thinking denies the possibility of thinking about the infant as having more complex emotional needs.

When parents are operating in non-mentalizing modes, it interferes with the possibility of the baby being known to their parents for whom they really are. They risk their baby experiencing an impingement on their sense of self, in as much as their real states and needs are not being recognized and understood. For a baby, who is so dependent on parental mirroring of their true state, this can feel catastrophic.

More than one of these non-mentalizing modes of thinking can be present at the same time, and they can also trigger each other. For example, a parent in a psychic equivalent mode might assume that their infant is behaving aggressively towards them; they may then (in pretend mode) start to think about how the infant is intending to upset them. These slightly overwhelming feelings about the negativity coming at them from the baby may lead the parent to act in a punitive manner – either towards the infant or him or herself.

The mentalizing domains

The four mentalizing domains describe different aspects of mentalizing activity, each of which can be understood as being on a continuum; good mentalizing means accessing these different activities and moving fluidly along each continuum. These domains, in terms of neurobiology, are quite distinct, being underpinned by different neural circuits. They are relevant to clinical practice because they allow us to understand the ways in which we think about mental states, and how we change the way we imagine what is happening according to different sets of circumstances. When a family is coming into assessment for PPIP, the therapist may detect that a parent is operating in one or more of the non-mentalizing modes. The therapist may also note the different mentalizing tendencies, or strengths and weaknesses of the parent, according to the following mentalizing domains.

Automatic–reflective mentalizing

Much of the everyday interaction between parent and infant relies on automatic mentalizing: responding intuitively to what the baby is communicating without much need for conscious thought. There will

however be moments when the parent's more conscious, reflective mentalizing is needed, for example when an unsettled, crying baby is not
easily soothed by ordinary caregiving behaviours and the parent needs to
think more deliberately about what might be causing the upset.

Self-other mentalizing

Such a difficult moment – perhaps a tired baby in the late afternoon
that the parent is struggling to soothe – will also call on the parent's
capacity to mentalize themselves: am I feeling tired and more irritable,
is this making me handle my baby less empathically, making my baby
even harder to settle? The mentalizing of the self as well as the other
is necessary to break the pattern of mutual upset in both parent and
infant. We have so far emphasized the importance of the parent's capacity to mentalize the infant. Equally important is the parent's ability to
make sense of their own mental states. Because of the intensely social
orientation of human cognition, self/other mentalizing can be quite
hard to disentangle (e.g., it seems that overlapping neural networks are
activated when mentalizing the self or others). But it is important to
keep in mind that when it comes to caring for young infants, the parent's capacity to mentalize themselves in the moment may need particular thought: the work at such points needs to be on the parent's state
of mind as much as the infant's. The infant's powerful affect and the fact
that the infant cannot help to regulate the parent's capacity to mentalize can lead the parent to lose sight of what they might be bringing to
the interaction and of the ability to differentiate between the infant's
state and their own state. A mentalizing perspective within PPIP might
involve seeking to recognize moments at which the parent's capacity
to mentalize themselves and thus self-regulate seems to collapse. This
often occurs in the face of the attachment needs or distress of the infant.

Cognitive-affective mentalizing

The example of the tired parent with the unsettled baby also highlights
the difference between cognitive and affective mentalizing. At some level,
we are referring here to the authenticity of the mentalizing act. Cognitive
mentalizing involves a "rational" approach in which mental states (again
in both oneself and others) can be named and labelled, but not necessarily
experienced emotionally. Excessive cognitive mentalizing can become a
form of pretend mode thinking (described earlier), in which thoughts and
feelings can be discussed and described, but without any genuine emotional core. It is safe to assume that an exhausted parent would not really be
able to soothe the child unless she was emotionally connected and feeling

empathy for her baby – this is affective mentalizing. But a parent who is stuck in an extreme form of affective mentalizing may become over-sensitive and over-reactive to an infant's emotional states. For example, the parent who struggles to soothe their baby may feel a failure every time the baby cries. The capacity of a parent to resonate with their infant's emotional experience but demonstrate that they are not consumed or destroyed by it is an important part of an infant's experience of feeling emotional safe with the parent and, as mentioned previously, is an aspect of mentalizing theory that draws upon Bion's concept of containment (Bion, 1963) and Winnicott's idea of holding (Winnicott, 1965). Maintaining a balance between cognitive and emotional mentalizing is also central to the parent's ability to continue the work of parenting without feeling drained, on the one hand, or cold and distanced, on the other hand.

Internal–external mentalizing

Finally, the parent's ability to soothe the baby involves making the leap from the external signs of the baby's distress to imagining the baby's internal experience. The parent would need to wonder if the baby at that moment is cold or wet (external states), or lonely and frightened (internal states). Excessive external mentalizing can lead to a focus on behaviours or over-reactions to cues, or a concrete focus on behaviours and their outcome – it can emerge as a teleological mode of non-mentalizing, that is, over-relying on overt behaviours in the infant when it comes to making sense of the infant's experience. Excessive internal mentalizing – when disconnected from external cues and environmental awareness – can result in "theories" about the infant's thoughts and feelings with an absence of mooring in reality. Much of the work of parenting is trying to decipher the external cues that a baby gives out, and to locate the source of distress or the focus of interest/desire whether that be externally or internally caused, or both at the same time. Is the infant hungry, is the way they are being held somehow uncomfortable, is their nappy rubbing, are they bored, lonely or in need reassurance after being startled? Any parent who focuses excessively on either internal or external explanations for their infant's distress will not easily be able to meet their needs.

The mentalizing dimensions help us to break down what is going on when it comes to understanding the mentalizing profile of a parent in relation to their infant. From a clinical perspective, we can see that a parent who tends to be more fixed at any one end of any of these continuums may struggle to recognize and meet their baby's needs, or may struggle to make sense of or regulate their own state of mind in relation to the baby. We will return to some of these ideas in later chapters in which we describe PPIP in practice.

Embodied mentalizing

When it comes to the infant's experience of being mentalized, non-verbal processes are crucial. Parental embodied mentalizing refers to the parent's capacity to implicitly conceive, comprehend, and extrapolate the infant's mental states from the infant's movement and expression, and adjust their own bodily responses accordingly. Of the four mentalizing domains, the dominant ones in embodied mentalizing are automatic, affective mentalizing, as opposed to cognitive and reflective. This is the very nature of embodied communication. Shai and Fonagy have written of embodied mentalizing:

> Because an infant's mind is very much based on bodily processes, actions and kinaesthetic feedback, a parent's embodied mentalizing is the chief means of achieving a meeting of minds with the infant. The process of assessing parental embodied mentalizing involves focussing precisely on such moments and examining the degree to which a parent's ability to appreciate his or her infant's kinaesthetically manifested mental state is translated into the parents, modifying her or his own kinesthetics in an attempt to fulfil the infant's intentions, even beyond the infant's own abilities.
>
> (Shai & Fonagy, 2013, p. 191)

Let us return to the experience of baby Amos, aged 3 months, whom we considered in Chapter 2. Here we will focus on the embodied interactions going on between Amos and his father, using some of the kinaesthetic qualities emphasized by Shai. Amos has been lying on his tummy for a few minutes and is beginning to fret – his body tenses, his face reddens, his head moves restlessly as he vocalizes negative affect. His father moves slowly down to his son's level (slow tempo, planned and composed pacing), forming a crouched, rounded position (fluent and restrained in terms of tension) as though a kinaesthetic embrace, and slowly brings his face close to his son's face. This embodied mentalizing is then complemented by verbal expressions of mentalizing, as he asks, in a gentle sing-song, "Whaaat's up? Are you getting sick of facing the blanket? Cooome on . . ." The father tucks his hand under Amos and says, "I'm going to give you a break".

A recent study of parental embodied mentalizing in relation to infants reported two interesting findings. The first was that embodied mentalizing and mind-mindedness (a measure of mentalizing that focuses on what the parent verbalizes to and about the infant) were positively correlated. Second, it was found that embodied mentalizing predicted secure attachment over and above the role of mind-minded speech (Shai & Meins, 2018). This is congruent with the baby's experience of the world being body-based.

Epistemic trust

One line of thinking that has recently come out of mentalizing theory deals with the idea of epistemic trust. Epistemic trust is defined as trust in the communication of information that humans need to form social bonds and function in a shared social world. This work is based on the work of developmental researchers Csibra and Gergely (Csibra & Gergely, 2006, 2009, 2011), who have argued that infants have a natural predisposition to learn from others; the infant's openness to learning from the parent is stimulated by the ostensive cues from the parent. By ostensive cues, we mean the behaviours that signify to the infant that the parent is communicating something of significance or particular interest, whether through eye contact, physical touch or "motherese". For example, a father invites his baby to participate in a game of clapping hands. Father joins and opens his hands and looks at the baby with an open smiling face, saying in a rhythmic voice, "clappy hands, clappy hands, shall we play clappy hands". The baby responds with excited kicking and hand movement, face open and expectant. Another father also initiates a hand-clapping game by instructing his baby, "clap hands, clap hands – this way!" This is communicated as an instruction rather than an invitation to the baby. Father's voice lacks the baby-oriented rhythms and melody (motherese) and playful facial expressions that constitute ostensive cues. His baby looks cautious and does not pick up the game, suggesting that he is not sure of the parent's intentions and that he cannot rely on prior social learning about the experience of play and the cues that proceed it. The first baby is learning from his parent that play can proceed with enjoyable turn-taking, and that joining with others is a source of pleasure and learning; the second baby may not be able to approach interactions with the same openness, he is showing that he does not anticipate that his father will be a rewarding playmate. This baby may miss out on some of the social learning associated with play. Such moments of interaction are so valuable to an infant because they create a moment of constructive shared attention – both players in the interaction are joining together to focus on a shared object, the game of clapping hands. Developmental and evolutionary psychologists are increasingly interested in this capacity for shared attention and co-mentalizing, sometime called the "we-mode", and what makes human cognitive development unique (Gallotti & Frith, 2013; O'Madagain & Tomasello, 2019; Tomasello, 2016).

Co-mentalizing is a form of interacting that involves quite a subtle and complicated arrangement where each person is aware of and can join with the other person's mind, but is also able to hold onto the idea that the other person's mind is separate and that their perspective is different, even while focusing on the same object. It has been suggested that social interactions that consistently and significantly make these moments of shared attention aversive, or when they are simply absent, potentially undermine the individual's capacity to develop a "we-mode". This in turn, can leave the individual somewhat cut off from the wealth of social and cultural sharing that provides emotional regulation, interpersonal connectedness and the ability to think and learn about one's own and other people's mental states (Fonagy et al., 2021). One of the tasks of PPIP is to enable parents and infants to join together in pleasurable shared attention, based on a curiosity about and investment in the other's mind. For example, this might be modelled by the therapist inviting the parent to join in we-mode in observing and thinking about the baby. Through such experiences the infant may learn that the human world is something that is worth engaging with and learning from, and that they are a valid part of this world. The parent can gain confidence as the "elder" who has something to communicate, and that they might initiate their baby into a wider world of social connectedness. This way of thinking about sharing states and connectedness brings to mind Stern's thinking about attunement (Stern, 1985). In considering the development of self in infancy, Stern emphasized the central developmental importance of attunement as a sharing of emotional states between infant and parent. From this experience the infant will develop the expectation that emotional states can be shared – an antidote to the experience and anticipation of aloneness and rejection. Perhaps attunement and shared attention can be seen as complementary aspects – emotional and cognitive – of development.

In the adult, lack of epistemic trust may make it more difficult to access therapeutic help. An internal survey at the Anna Freud Centre showed that families who were referred by a trusted health visitor for PPIP tended to engage with the therapy more than families referred by a professional they did not know, where they felt they were simply being passed on. Lack of epistemic trust may also influence the relationship with the therapist as a source of relevant social information. For example, a therapist's comments on the baby's interest in her mummy might be seen as irrelevant and passed over, or may be dismissed as inaccurate – "the baby wasn't looking at me, she was looking at the picture behind me", or taken as a criticism – "I don't need you to tell me what my baby is doing". Developing trust within the therapeutic relationship may take time and is highly dependent on the therapist. Mentalizing treatment has developed a particular stance, a way of thinking and interacting, that works to create the conditions in which openness to learning about and from other minds is generated.

The mentalizing stance

Across all the different forms of MBT, one of the core ideas is that we cannot know what mental states are with absolute certainty. The mentalizing stance is an authentic attitude of curiosity about what is going on in someone's mind. This involves getting to know about these states and managing them in oneself so they serve our interactions and life constructively (Bateman & Fonagy, 2016). The response to a collapse in mentalizing, particularly if it occurs alongside heightened affect, is not to mentalize for or at the patient, but rather to create a process of open curiosity in which the therapist models their own lack of certainty about, and their authentic interest in, mental states. The PPIP therapist works to enhance the mentalizing system generated by infant and parent, by holding a mentalizing stance in relation to all partners in the interaction in an empathic, non-judgemental, openly curious and authentic manner.

Mentalizing and interpreting

In psychoanalytic terms, interpretation seeks to elucidate aspects of the internal world that are not currently in the person's consciousness, but may be helpful in building understanding of his or her functioning. An example of an interpretation in PPIP may be to make links between a parent's negative attribution to their infant and their past history, "perhaps the way he (the baby) looks at you reminds you of your mother's stony stares which made you feel so diminished". The mentalizing stance is primarily a questioning one, posing what has been described as "what questions", rather than the "why questions" that are implied in an interpretation. In this example, it might involve asking about the parent's feelings and thoughts at that moment and what the thought process was that led to that feeling, and wondering about other perspectives on their child's state of mind. Bateman and Fonagy describe the process thus:

> Whilst we might point to similarities in patterns of relationship in therapy and in childhood, or currently outside of the therapy, the aim of this is not to provide the patients with an explanation (insight) that they might be able to use to control their behaviour pattern, but

far more simply to highlight one other puzzling phenomenon that requires thought and contemplation.

(Bateman & Fonagy, 2010, p. 10)

The issue of interpretation versus inquiry is one in where mentalizing has influenced PPIP: there is greater recognition of the importance of building mentalizing capacities, sometimes before and sometimes alongside offering insight.

References

Bateman, A., & Fonagy, P. (2010). Mentalization based treatment for borderline personality disorder. *World Psychiatry*, *9*(1), 11–15.

Bateman, A., & Fonagy, P. (2016). *Mentalization-based treatment for personality disorders: A practical guide*. Oxford, UK: Oxford University Press.

Bateman, A., & Fonagy, P. (Eds.). (2019). *Handbook of mentalizing in mental health practice* (2nd ed.). Washington, DC: American Psychiatric Publishing.

Bion, W. R. (1963). *Elements of psycho-analysis*. London, UK: Heinemann.

Csibra, G., & Gergely, G. (2006). Social learning and social cognition: The case for pedagogy. In M. H. Johnson & Y. Munakata (Eds.), *Processes of change in brain and cognitive development: Attention and Performance XXI* (pp. 249–274). Oxford, UK: Oxford University Press.

Csibra, G., & Gergely, G. (2009). Natural pedagogy. *Trends in Cognitive Sciences*, *13*(4), 148–153. doi:10.1016/j.tics.2009.01.005

Csibra, G., & Gergely, G. (2011). Natural pedagogy as evolutionary adaptation. *Philosophical Transactions of the Royal Society of London: Series B, Biological Sciences*, *366*(1567), 1149–1157. doi:10.1098/rstb.2010.0319

Fonagy, P., Campbell, C., Constantinou, M., Higgitt, A., Allison, E., & Luyten, P. (2021). Culture and psychopathology. *Development and Psychopathology*, 1–16. doi:10.1017/S0954579421000092

Fonagy, P., Gergely, G., Jurist, E., & Target, M. (2002). *Affect regulation, mentalization, and the development of the self*. New York, NY: Other Press.

Fonagy, P., & Target, M. (1996). Playing with reality: I. Theory of mind and the normal development of psychic reality. *International Journal of Psycho-Analysis*, 77(Pt 2), 217–233.

Fotopoulou, A., & Tsakiris, M. (2017). Mentalizing homeostasis: The social origins of interoceptive inference. *Neuropsychoanalysis*, *19*(1), 3–28. doi:10.1080/1529414 5.2017.1294031

Gallotti, M., & Frith, C. D. (2013). Social cognition in the we-mode. *Trends in Cognitive Sciences*, *17*, 160–165. doi:10.1016/j.tics.2013.02.002

Luyten, P., Campbell, C., Allison, E., & Fonagy, P. (2020). The mentalizing approach to psychopathology: State of the art and future directions. *Annual Review of Clinical Psychology*, *16*, 297–325. doi:10.1146/annurev-clinpsy-071919-015355

O'Madagain, C., & Tomasello, M. (2019). Joint attention to mental content and the social origin of reasoning. *Synthese*. doi:10.1007/s11229-019-02327-1

Shai, D., & Belsky, J. (2011). Parental embodied mentalizing: Let's be explicit about what we mean by implicit. *Child Development Perspectives*, *5*(3), 187–188.

Shai, D., & Fonagy, P. (2013). Beyond words: Parental embodied mentalizing and the parent–infant dance. In M. Mikulincer & P. R. Shaver (Eds.), *Mechanisms of social connection from brain to group* (pp. 185–203). Washington, DC: American Psychological Association.

Shai, D., & Meins, E. (2018). Parental embodied mentalizing and its relation to mind-mindedness, sensitivity, and attachment security. *Infancy*, *23*, 857–872. doi:10.1111/infa.12244

Stern, D. N. (1985). *The interpersonal world of the infant: A view from psychoanalysis and developmental psychology*. New York, NY: Basic Books.

Tomasello, M. (2016). *A natural history of human morality*. Cambridge, MA: Harvard Univ Press.

Winnicott, D. W. (1965). The theory of the parent-infant relationship (1960). In *The maturational process and the facilitating environment* (pp. 37–55). London, UK: Hogarth Press.

6 The PPIP and mentalizing model in practice

In this chapter the focus is on the practice of psychoanalytic parent-infant psychotherapy with a commentary from a mentalizing perspective. To reiterate, traditionally in work with parents and infants mentalizing practice would focus on the parental mind. The infant's communications, affects and attention would be explored with the parent, but the infant would not be addressed directly as a patient as such. Therefore, we discuss overlaps and difference between the PPIP and mentalization approaches via detailed exploration of how PPIP is implemented.

We will begin with a discussion of the factors we take into consideration when assessing whether PPIP might be a suitable form of help for parent/parents and infant. We then describe aspects of the clinical processes that are unique to this modality of treatment. This begins with planning the physical setting, the process of managing the inclusion of both parent/parents and infant as partners and patients, balancing the needs of all participants and ways of working with parents, infants and their relationship. Clinical vignettes will illustrate working with strengths, difficulties and risk in different situations. Throughout, we include the mind of the therapist as part of the process.

Suitability

Families seek help from PPIP for a range of reasons. They might find becoming or being a parent hard to cope with or experience difficult feelings that have been stirred up by the conception, pregnancy and birth. They may be worried about their relationship with their baby or concerned about their baby's development; or, as an adoptive parent, they may be seeking support in developing their relationship with their baby. Certain situations and conditions are also known to place particular strains on the parent-infant relationship, such as postnatal depression and other mental health issues, socio-economic stress or domestic violence.

DOI: 10.4324/9781003024323-6

When it comes to clinical considerations in the assessment of fit between the PPIP modality and the family, the PPIP model does not require a formal assessment process of the family. Suitability for PPIP is established through an experience of being and working together during the initial meeting or meetings. In these meetings, both the conscious goals of treatment and the more unconscious difficulties and aspirations should become apparent. These will be discussed and unless there are counterindications to this way of working, one of which is client preference, there is agreement to continue therapy. Where there are doubts – whether on the part of the parents or therapist (these doubts do usually coincide, but not always) – there is a review. The parents may decide to withdraw or, perhaps a more helpful outcome for some, may accept a referral to another service.

There are some pointers as to whether PPIP treatment might be helpful for the family. These may be associated with one or more of the following:

- States of mind in a parent that impinge on their "good enough" parenting capacities. For example, unresolved mourning (e.g., of own parent), a traumatic birth, unprocessed childhood relational trauma in the parent.
- Unconscious behaviours such as frightening and anomalous behaviours (see Adaptation and defence in Chapter 3) in the presence of, and/or towards, the baby.
- Parental difficulties in assuming the role of parent in relation to the state of infancy. For example, difficulties in tolerating the immediacy of their infant's dependency, vulnerability and neediness.
- Bonding issues, as when a parent does not feel that their baby is theirs or feels that the baby dislikes them.
- Parental difficulties in mentalizing their baby, such that the infant is not related to as a separate person with age-appropriate needs and developmental tasks, or the infant's state of mind/feelings are conspicuously misjudged.
- Frequent and/or persistent heightened negative arousal in the parent-infant interactions. This is especially challenging when parent and infant trigger each other's distress, creating a cycle of negative interactions that the parent struggles to break.
- Signs of developmental stress/distress in the infant, such as low mood, physical passivity, withdrawal, persistent or frequent dysregulation of physical and/or emotional states, including feeding and sleeping difficulties.

Parents who may be more receptive to PPIP are often those who can engage with the idea that mental states are meaningful and to whom it intuitively makes sense that meaning underpins behaviour. These parents may be more able to imagine that they and their baby are in a relationship that involves interactive emotional communication. Parents who do not start off with this capacity for mentalizing may still show curiosity in the therapist's thinking or ideas – for example, the suggestion that the parent's states of mind may impact their infant, or that their infant is triggering strong reactions in them that perhaps belong elsewhere. What we have also learned is that some parents may be able to mentalize themselves but not their babies. In such instances, the therapist must assess whether a space can be created in the parent's mind for the baby as a subject in his or her own right.

Suitability for PPIP may also be linked to what the parents hope treatment will help with, as recent studies have highlighted links between expectations of treatment and outcomes. Salomonsson and Sandell found that mothers who actively wanted to partake in psychoanalytic exploration and who indicated that they understood that they somehow have contributed to the present problems within the mother-infant relationship benefitted most from the therapy and improved in their maternal interactive sensitivity with their babies post treatment (Salomonsson & Sandell, 2011a, 2011b). This group comprised the chaotic, the depressed/reserved and the uncertain mothers. Those who seemed to benefit less from the psychoanalytic approach were categorized as the "abandoned" mothers – this group felt abandoned either because their partners had left them, or, more subtly, because they felt that their needs were impossible to meet in the face of the competing needs of the infant.

A similar study – more specifically focused on PPIP at the Anna Freud – found that improved parental reflective function, that is, the capacity to mentalize, was predicted by participants' pre-treatment expectations that their parent-infant relationship would improve through the treatment (Ransley, Sleed, Baradon, & Fonagy, 2019). These parents indicated their awareness of a problem in the relationship with their baby and a wish to change this. Interestingly, this same group of parents also, in parallel, expressed concerns about discussing their past experiences. The authors wondered whether the concern around discussing their past may be indicative of a greater pre-existing awareness, perhaps intuitive, in relation to the impact on them of their past experiences. In other words, mothers who wanted to better their relationship with their baby, particularly perhaps if against a background of childhood trauma, seemed to increase their mentalizing capacities in therapy. This is congruent with a wish, frequently expressed by PPIP parents who have suffered emotional privation, that their children should have a better childhood than they had.

There are also parental features that are clinically associated with limited benefit from PPIP treatment and/or early drop out. These are mainly to do with ways the parents view relationships and issues associated with intimacy, such as trust and dependency, and the defences they use to protect themselves from anxieties to do with such relationships. For example, parents who are dismissive of the importance of attachments, or who simply do not have concerns about themselves or their baby, or who consistently hold others responsible for any difficulties that occur, may be protecting themselves by using mental mechanisms such as denial, disavowal and projection. Such parents may be able to benefit from adult MBT in terms of their own functioning but may still struggle to parent the baby.

Patterns of attachment and defence that negate mutuality and intersubjectivity, blocking the meaningful focus on the parent–infant relationship, may point to entrenched epistemic mistrust (see Chapter 5). Such a position can manifest as overt hostility, fear or scepticism about engaging with authority figures, making it hard for the parent to join forces with the therapist to be helped. But distortions in the capacity to engage with and "learn from" the therapist can be more subtle. As mentioned earlier, Salomonsson and Sandell found that mothers who had a pervasive need to be taken care of were less likely to benefit (Salomonsson & Sandell, 2011b). This may be understood, perhaps, in terms of an inability to tolerate need and dependency in their babies when their own sense of relational deprivation is so deep. The PPIP approach of holding the baby in mind may be experienced as failing yet again to acknowledge a powerful aspect of their own experience and need. A parent's difficulty in sharing the therapeutic space with his or her infant creates a dilemma because the infant's needs are a reality that cannot be put on hold but are, inevitably, ongoing and urgent demands in the here-and-now, as described in Chapter 2. The therapist will, therefore, be asking if such parental features can shift within the infant's developmental timetable.

Finally, in terms of engagement with a therapeutic process, whether or not it is thought that PPIP may be helpful to the parent/parents and infant depends on the parent's potential to:

- Attend sessions regularly.
- Form a potentially trusting relationship with therapist.
- Acknowledge their difficulties and show some willingness to think about own states.
- Accept that their state and behaviours have an impact on their baby.
- Share the therapeutic space of the therapist's attention with his or her infant.
- Tolerate the therapist's interventions.
- Carry-over understanding of concerns from one session to the next.
- Set treatment goals that are inclusive of the baby.

It must be acknowledged, however, that it is not always possible in early sessions to assess a parent's capacity for change, or whether the changes will meet the baby's developmental timetable. Sometimes taking on a family for PPIP is a matter of faith rather than evidence.

The physical setting

Entering a PPIP therapeutic space offers a particular experience of holding. The physical setting aims to be inclusive of the adults and baby. A carpet (or blanket) on the floor, in the centre of which a baby mat is set out with a few age-appropriate toys and, where possible, large cushions around the mat, set the scene for immersive being-with the baby. From the baby's point of view, the "village" ("it takes a village to raise a baby") surrounds him/her. It demarcates the generations, in which parents and therapists are the adults. It also places the therapist as an active participant alongside the parents and seeks to convey to them that they are not alone in their task of caring and thinking about their baby's needs. This arrangement conveys in physical terms a model of togetherness that positions the parent-infant relationship as the crucible of the work (Baradon, Biseo, Broughton, James, & Joyce, 2016).

Where the treatment is offered within a home setting, it is important to try to carve out a boundaried space within the room in which the therapy takes place. However, the ordinary setting of the room may conflict with the frame we aim to achieve, inasmuch as the adults may sit on chairs or sofa, the baby may not be in the middle, a television may be on. In other circumstances, such as the work in hostels, the family may inhabit one room. Even there, to the extent possible, a physical frame is created with the parent/parents which represents the stance and way-of-working in this model.

The therapeutic contract

Introducing parents to the PPIP model is different from setting the frame in other modalities inasmuch as it is a mixed infant and adult-led space, involving emotional, embodied reverberations with infantile states. A number of features are distinct to the therapeutic contract in PPIP.

The first is that the therapy is about the relationship between the parents and their baby/the baby and his or her parents. Expectations that the therapy will be for either the parent ("I need help") or the baby ("she is the problem") have to be reframed. Experientially this means that parental material is, of course, sometimes the focus but it is, in the end result, referenced to their parenting and the baby's experience. In the same vein, while attention is sometimes on the baby and his or her inner world, it is contextualized by the view that "there is no baby without a mother" and/or father – and development is relational. An illustration may clarify this central tenet of the work:

MOTHER: She cries unless held . . . I can't stand it

THERAPIST (interested voice): Tell me more [Th glances at M and at B, indicating that the question is addressed to both]

M: She is such a clingy baby

TH: And her clinginess makes you feel? [adult focused question]

M: Suffocated [makes a movement of pushing away with her hand, and sighs}

TH: Mm

TH [looking at Baby, speaking softly]: Is that what happens? You NEED to hold on to mummy sometimes? And then mummy can't breathe, and can't hold you. And then? Do you cry inside you, "mummy, mummy"? Do you just go to sleep? [infant focused question]

    TH (looks at M, eyebrows raised, questioning expression on her face)

M: I try not to show her how I feel

TH: I'm sure

M [after sad pause]: Yes, she cries and it all goes wrong

In this vignette the therapist alternates her attention between mother's experience and baby's. What links these two foci is that she is attending to both individuals and to their relationship by explicitly holding both in mind throughout. This inclusive and flexible stance is introduced in the first phone call, in which the involvement of baby (always) and partner (if available and willing) is established. When the family comes for their first meeting and thereafter, the parents and baby are greeted by name. A personal greeting to the baby is aimed to establish him/her as an equal participant in the process, just as the baby mat indicates his/her central place. Evidencing the ongoing dual or triadic focus is then part and parcel of the therapist's interventions. Sometimes this position is not explicit, and at times may be compromised and need recalibrating. It is important to keep in mind the presence, absence and quality of the therapist's "split vision" – one eye on the parent and one eye on the baby, and a third observing their back and forth. For example, while speaking with the parent, the therapist may keep her gaze on the baby. Or, her glance may move rapidly between baby and parent. S/he may position herself opposite the parent or alongside them. S/he may interrupt the flow: "Can we hold this conversation in mind but just stop a moment to attend to Baby . . ." or (to baby) "I know you also want to play but daddy is just telling me something SO important to him, can you wait one more moment?" In such moments it is very important not to lose track of the conversation or play that has been punctuated so that what is put on hold is not lost, tolerance of frustration is rewarded and trust in the therapist's ability to hold two or more people in mind is reinforced.

Beginning the session

How the family settles into the space of the consulting room or the designated therapy space in their home sometimes gives an immediate indication of the nature of the difficulties in the parent-infant relationship. The following is an example in which the dyad's trauma unfolded very quickly in the first session.

> Mother places four-month-old Grace carefully on the floor, facing herself and away from the therapist. She gives her a little smile as though to reassure her, yet Grace's gaze remains fixed to right of her mother's face, so there is no eye contact between them.

The therapist immediately picked up on Grace's avoidant gaze: she kept her eyes averted from mother for what seemed a long time under the circumstances of being in a new place, with a new person. What could it mean? Was she expressing a bodily expectation that she needs to hold herself together and should not look for succour from her mother? This would suggest that mother was not experienced as a comforting presence, a secure base when faced with a stranger in unfamiliar surroundings. The therapist wondered whether avoidance was a generalized feature – perhaps explaining Grace's seeming "lack of interest" in herself – the stranger, and the new environment. Was she too anxious? Was she inhibiting expectable anxiety and/or interest?

> The therapist waits as mother adjusts herself on floor. Mother seemed child-like in her big-eyed meekness and the way she seemed to settle herself for presentation to the other (therapist).

The therapist wondered what transference the mother brought to this first meeting. Was her docility an attempt to appease a potentially dangerous person in her mind? And perhaps Grace's anxious bodily rigidity expressed this transference of her mother to the therapist as a threat? It was also possible that Mother was shamed by Grace's seeming "rejection" of her, as though she exposed her failure as a parent. Within minutes of meeting mother and infant, the therapist had learnt about their loneliness in relation to each other and, potentially, in relation to her. This vignette reconstructs the therapist's immediate impressions in the first minutes of the first encounter and her roaming mind, seeking the meaning of the observed behaviours and affects. It also shows the therapist's wish to give the mother and baby time to "unfold" in their own ways.

When Mother had settled, the therapist opened up a space: "tell me about yourselves and why you are here". Such open questions position the parent as the agent of their story; the content, the manner in which it is delivered and its coherence will inform the therapist of the parent's state of mind.

MOTHER SAID: I just don't want to be like my mother to Grace. She was really violent, she made me feel worthless, which I still do. I just don't feel for her (Grace) as much as I should, or I love her, but I can't show her, I'm scared to in case she's horrible to me when she grows up.

The therapist registered that a complex abuser-abused relationship was already repeating intergenerationally with Mother and her baby. In Mother's mind, Grace (at 4 months) seemed to represent the grand-maternal abuser. This was Mother's transference to her infant. But there was also some awareness that she could become like her own mother, unable to provide love in mothering of Grace. While this conversation took place, the therapist watched for Grace's communications about her own state of mind and held a "double agenda" (Cramer, 1998), listening to what Mother was saying and observing what Grace did that shed light on her mother's unconscious communication. She surmised that Grace's avoidance spoke to the hostility in Mother towards her as an actual, and not only potential, abuser.

A mentalizing therapist might have opened the session with the same question, but would have responded differently to Mother's reply. The hypotheses made earlier by the PPIP therapist would not come into a mentalizing response. For example, the intergenerational story would be relevant in as much as it seemed to interfere with the mother's thoughts about her infant's state. The mother's response would have cued the therapist to focus initially on the mother's dilemma in the moment, "it must be hard to see your baby and see those things from your mother in her". The experience of being thought about in this way is considered a way of opening (epistemic) trust and creating the conditions in which mental states feel safe to explore. This would enable a move to introduce another perspective, in this case, to mentalize her baby's experience, "I wonder if you can imagine what Grace could be feeling at the moment?"

> The session progressed with Mother telling the therapist more about her background and the damage she felt it had done to her. She listed the many troubled times she had experienced, including abandonment by Grace's father when he learned she was pregnant. While she was talking, she prepared Grace for a feed. Grace sucked briefly, seemingly hungry, then choked and started crying inconsolably. Suddenly she slipped into a frozen state – eyes rolling.

The unfolding events were shocking to witness. It seemed that Grace's choking was a communication about her experience and not only a physiological hitch of choking and becoming frustrated. What was striking was that this ordinarily difficult interaction became, for Mother and Grace (who had no physical difficulties in relation to feeding such as tongue-tie), a moment of acute and spiralling distress, in which Mother appeared defeated and the baby inconsolable. The milk, to the therapist, represented mother's trauma – unverbalized, unprocessed, but alive in mother's body and deposited into Grace with her feed. Her crying conveyed desperate anxiety and, in the face of fragmentation, she dissociated (frozen state and eyes rolling). This particularly heightened first session demonstrates the extent to which the PPIP therapist has to be prepared to receive and contain trauma in both mother and infant at any point in the therapy.

From a mentalizing perspective, we might see this moment of crisis in the interaction as arising out of Mother's emotional arousal in response to Grace's upset, causing a collapse in her own capacity to mentalize. In particular she was unable to distinguish between her own and Grace's mental states – perhaps in a sense Mother, too, was crying desperately inside, and was thus unable to regulate either herself or her baby.

Working with strengths

As discussed, work with the parent seeks to reinforce interactions where the parent cares well enough for his or her baby alongside addressing difficulties in the relationship. Working with the strengths of the parents and baby positions the therapist as ally with the healthy part of parental and infant functioning, as well as witness to their success. With this mother, it was possible to genuinely speak to her capacity for concern for her baby, which she demonstrated in bringing the two of them to therapy, showing an interest in why things were as they were, and trying to provide for her in the session. The aim with regards to the baby is to keep attachment pathways open through the mutual rewards of responsive parenting: the therapist helps the parent to respond and to observe and accept their baby's "appreciation" (smiles, seeking out eye contact, ceasing to cry). In some instances, the therapist may be more directly active with the baby when the parent is unable to do so, to keep alive in the baby the expectation that an available adult will be on hand to respond. The following are some of the approaches the therapist was able to use with Mother and Grace in later sessions: observing and mirroring ("Did you notice how Grace smiled at you when you spoke now?"), recalibrating mentalizing ("you describe a dip in a long busy day with her, help me understand how the two parts – the caring and the dip – fit together in your mind"), interpretation of, for example, stringent self-criticism ("I can hear how harsh that voice inside is, so critical of the care you do give"), a reminder of reciprocity in development ("she needs you to accept her joy in having you as her mother"). Reinforcing Baby's revitalized attempts to capture her mother's attention ("call mummy again, Grace, she didn't hear you") and representing her communications to her mother ("do you think . . . maybe, you know, she is saying she doesn't want more milk, just to play with you as you hold her") also help to highlight and support strengths in the parent-infant relationship.

Revisiting past trauma

When to take up what patient material is, of course, a perennial dilemma in any therapy. In relation to intergenerational transmission of trauma and PPIP, the dilemma additionally presents in making judgements about to whose trauma – parent's or baby's – the therapist should attend. And which trauma, the past or present? In the tradition of Fraiberg and her colleagues (Fraiberg, Adelson, & Shapiro, 1975), parental trauma is seen as the port of entry in transforming traumatizing interactions between parent and infant, and this thinking remains central to the PPIP model. However, we have learned to be cautious about exploring the parent's past as a matter of course. Many parents experience the empathic understanding of their past as a relief from feelings of helplessness and shame, and grow from it to develop greater epistemic trust in relationships (e.g., with the therapist) and more responsive relating with their baby. In psychoanalytic terms we see this psychological processing and integration in the parent as involving the withdrawal of projections and the emergence of the ability to see the baby as baby. However, there are some parents who are re-traumatized by probing these memories, and others – perhaps more dismissive in their attachment style – for whom dwelling on traumatic attachments makes no sense and in fact can arouse resistance. Thus, while the therapist's thinking invariably includes hypotheses about those aspects of the parent's past which may be an impediment to current parenting, we have found that the most fruitful interventions are often those that originate in observed traumatizing transactions between parent and infant in the here-and-now, and which also capture the immediacy of the baby's experience.

Examples of this would be times when mother withdrew helplessly from Grace, or when her cries ended in dissociation, or she choked on her bottle or hit herself with a toy. The therapeutic conversations sometimes remained with Grace's experiences in relation to expectable, age-appropriate expressions. At other times, therapist and mother explored Mother's memories of her experiences with her parents, and possible links between these and difficulties between her and her baby. Attempts were made to help Mother think about the present and past and the transgenerational experiences in a more mentalizing way, so that the grip of trauma in her and Grace's relationship could be loosened. Classical psychoanalytic technique involves working more directly with the patient's transference to the therapist (Tuckett, 2019), but both mentalizing and PPIP have developed a more subtle approach to the use of transference. In PPIP work, the therapist will be constantly thinking about the transference and countertransference processes that may be at play at any given moment, but transference interpretations are given cautiously and lightly when they relate to him/herself. The emphasis remains primarily on the moment-to-moment interaction between parent and infant and transferences *to the baby* that may be impacting their relating. In mentalizing-informed approaches, past-present transference interpretations are given less space than the how and what of inter-relational processes, in order to think about them in mentalizing terms. In that sense, both mentalizing and PPIP therapists show particular interest in exploring jointly created interactions as they unfold and where the emotions may be most live or most defended against.

Working directly with the baby

Work with the baby takes place in a mixture of verbal and embodied languages. This is illustrated in the following vignettes:

Family A

Baby Muhammed and his mother were referred 2 months after mother tripped while holding him, then age 2 months, and Muhammed fell from her arms to the ground. Although reassured that no medical damage had occurred Mother was beset by overwhelming anxiety that she could not care safely for her baby. This had the quality of rumination.

In an early session in the therapy, Muhammed slipped sideways from the cushion against which he had been propped. He landed gently on the soft carpet and looked around from his new position with an expression of surprise and puzzlement.

Mother gasped and cried out "Oh OH look" (to therapist) "Are you alright" (to the baby). She picked him up and cradled him and Muhammed cried loudly. A while later mother and baby were sufficiently settled and he was placed once more on the baby mat. As he settled, the therapist leaned towards him and nodded her head, saying in motherese: "you went slippety slip, slippety slip (moving her head in rhythm with the chant) and you landed on the mat . . . and you weren't sure: was it a b-i-g fall or was it a little slip? Were you very (deeper voice) shocked and frightened or just a little bit (high pitched softer voice) surprised?" Therapist looked at Muhammed enquiringly, with a slight smile, and he looked at the therapist and then at Mother. The therapist, too, looked at Mother and gave a small shrug.

The therapist here seems to be setting the scene for distinguishing between the two events that are different in scale of danger and anxiety. The therapist wonders whether Muhammed would have conflated the events (fall-from-mother's-arms and slipperty-slip from the cushion) were Mother not so hyper-aroused and, therefore, more able to clarify and contain his response. In the first instance, the therapist addresses Muhammed's actual experience in the moment: slippety slip resulting in a soft landing. She does this primarily with her tone of voice, the melody of her speech, her facial expressions and head movements. These vitality affects (Stern, 1985) scaffold her words. She then adds verbalization of the emotional dimension, and the confusion: was it a big anxiety or a manageable dose of surprise. In her own mind the therapist also wonders about Mother's decision to prop Muhammed up when he is manifestly and age-appropriately still unstable. She wonders whether Mother needs to re-enact the fall in her (the therapist's) presence in order to master that trauma. With this mental preoccupation with Mother she is primed to follow Muhammed's lead in looking at her. His move opens the way for the therapist's next intervention, which is inclusive of both.

Therapist (to Muhammed): "I think that mummy was also unsure, yeah . . . and both of you are maybe a bit stuck together in that body-feeling from The-Big-Fall [forceful enunciation]".

The therapist is naming the conscious organizing event: The Big Fall, to mark its multilayered body-feeling significance. She mentions being "stuck", referring to Mother's ruminative thinking accompanied by overwhelming anxiety This stuckness may be older than the fall, she thinks, but does not yet open up this question for discussion. She also suggests that the stuckness is a shared state; it is, in her thinking, underpinned by Muhammed's infantile vulnerability.

Therapist, to mother in an adult voice, empathic: "I guess terrible guilt is triggered too?"

> Mother nods, eyes filling with tears. She strokes her baby's cheeks softly and gives him a little smile.

An example of a more embodied intervention with a different baby occurred in a first session with a young, asylum-seeking couple.

Family B

The family arrived early for their appointment and therapist heard the very young baby, Raya, crying for a length of time in the waiting room. She felt worried and aroused. Upon entering the consulting room, she saw the father, who was carrying the baby, lower Raya to the floor as though a package. Crouching down, the therapist brought her face closer to Raya's face and crooned "hello little person". She nodded and smiled gently; the baby's eyes fixed on her. The therapist continued this musical multi-modal engagement with the baby – using her face, proximity, voice, movement – as the parents moved around, placing bags and coats and choosing where to sit. She then welcomed them and personalized Raya further by calling her by name.

We note the therapists' split-second decisions as to where to focus attention. In the first vignette (Muhammed and his mother) the therapist verbalized the shared question for both baby and mother. In the second vignette (Raya and her parents) the therapist responded with urgency to the "non-personalized" vacuum around the baby with a dedicated attempt to create an experience of intersubjectivity with the baby to bring her life. Indeed, with experience, therapists learn to make instantaneous decisions guided by the precept of "what will further the goal of strengthening the relationship between parent and infant?", "How can I help these parents claim this baby?", "How can the baby be supported to claim his parents?" Yet, as research has shown, these "decisions" are often less conscious than we may think (Avdi & Seikkula, 2019); rather they derive from "pre-reflective" bodily knowledge that has accrued with therapeutic experience. The choice of where/what to attend to determines "who/ what is the patient" at any given moment in a session.

Play, playfulness and the use of toys

Many parents attending PPIP say that they do not know how to play with their baby. By this they mean that they do not know how to be a playmate with their baby, and how to move from presenting a toy to the infant to playing with the infant and the toys in an inclusive way. Often this self-observation arises after they have watched the therapist interacting playfully with the baby. One aspect of play with a baby that may be new to the parent/parents is to follow the baby's lead and open up the play through turn-taking. Another new experience for the parent may be the use of self or toys in a more symbolic way. For example, a therapist played peekaboo with a 6-month baby whose mother has just gone back to work. She used her hands to hide her face and then emerge – greeting the baby with a big hello of rediscovery. With another baby she used a baby teddy who came and disappeared "like daddy does", expressing confusion and loss when "daddy bear" was gone. Helping a parent play may entail modelling or actively including the parent in the play – particularly with a parent whose own childhood had lacked playfulness. A parent may feel frightened by potential emotional laxity when play takes place through exaggerated face-to-face interactions, or the apparent chaos of cars flying in and out of sight as a way of mastering separation.

   Sometimes, interpretation is helpful:
   Therapist was trying to draw out a subdued 7-month-old. She gently hopped a little red block to the baby and paused it near her foot to say a whispering "hello". Mother said: "I never do that. I don't know how to". The therapist hopped the red block to the baby's hand, whispering "hello again". With her eyes still on the baby and holding the interaction with baby through a quizzical expression on her face (expressing the question "will you join me, baby, or not?"), she said to mother: "Perhaps there was no space inside you to pretend when you were a child. You were too busy looking out for threats". The therapist turned to look at mother, who nodded. A few minutes later mother picked up another block, blue in colour, and examined it. Then put it down. "Mmm", mused the therapist, addressing neither baby nor mother specifically, "I wonder if the blue block also wants to play?" Mother hesitantly hopped the block. The therapist moved her block towards mother's and said, in the same tone, "hello, shall we visit Baby?"

In this example playfulness was a means to engage both baby and mother with the therapist, and through her – with each other. Mother-the-adult was enabled to experiment with playful aspects of her mind that had been inhibited during her childhood. Playfulness requires the ability to hold another perspective with a foothold in qualities of pleasure, fun, connectivity. Such freedom was not available to this mother in her own childhood, during which she was surrounded by threat. The PPIP therapist, in actively communicating with the infant, is seeking to give both parent and infant an experience of being in a shared imaginary world, demonstrating to the infant that there is an interest in joining up with his/her mind – a person to be mentalized. Play is a natural medium for such socialization.

Older babies are provided with age-appropriate toys. The selection of toys reflects individual preferences and the baby's capacity to use the toys for his or her developmental needs. These may be physical – such as practising the manipulation of objects, or psychological. For example, a doll's bottle and bowl may be put out for a baby who is beginning to wean; containers can be helpful to a pre-toddler who is beginning to be curious about inside and outside, internal and external.

Rhythms and ending

As in all therapies, a certain rhythm builds up over time, with a beginning, middle and end to each session, and this anchors the baby and the parents as the predictability can help to provide a sense of containment. But during the session there are often of peaks and troughs in emotional regulation as raw emotions arise and then are, hopefully, worked through. In the early part of therapy providing this containment may fall to the therapist, in relation to both parent/parents and baby. This may also be part of the rhythm in each session. One of the features of progress in a session, and in the therapy overall, is that the regulating role of the therapist is taken over by the parent in relation both to self and ministering to the baby. And it is not only in relation to emotional regulation that greater agency is assumed by the parent. When therapy is going well, parents claim their position as the person who know best what their baby is feeling and "saying", and how to respond.

Ending a session needs forethought and preparation. The parent must leave in a sufficiently integrated state to resume full care of the baby without the therapist's support. Parents who have difficulty being alone with their baby may feel the loss of the therapist's physical presence acutely as they leave the room. Or perhaps particularly upsetting material has come up in the session and the therapeutic space has cocooned the parent and baby, leaving the dyad feeling exposed and vulnerable when it is time to leave. At other times, perhaps there might be anger or conflict that does not feel adequately resolved when the session comes to an end. Babies get used to receiving attention, understanding, containing and play from the session. They may be reluctant to leave a safe and stimulating space. Infant protest can be taxing on the parent ("she only does this here!!") and perhaps arousing if the parent, too, feels prematurely "thrown out". Little rituals can be introduced to scaffold the departure for the baby and parent alike – putting toys away, comparing diaries. This can be helpful in creating structures especially in families where there is lack of preparation for the next action or event of the day.

Risk during or at the close of a session

On the rare occasions a therapist and/or parent may feel it is not safe for them to leave, and external supports may have to be called upon. This may be the other parent of the child, grandparents or social services. An example of such a scenario is described here:

> A highly ambivalent mother came to a session, 9 months into therapy, in an agitated state after an argument with a neighbour. Her little boy, Rio, usually quite boisterous, was subdued. Mother related the details of the exchange and, at an 'inopportune' moment, Rio started whining. Mother leapt to her feet and, standing over him – towering over him – screamed: "I hate being your mother". Therapist and Rio were shocked, and mother probably too. When emotions had calmed somewhat the therapist probed mother's feelings about going home with Rio: the journey home, opening the front door, stepping into the apartment, having to prepare lunch. Mother felt it would not be manageable. With the mother's consent, and in her presence, the therapist called social services and between the three adults (mother, social worker on the phone, therapist) there was agreement that father would be contacted and until he arrived mother and Rio would stay at the Centre.

Post–session reflectivity and supervision

As evident from the vignettes, PPIP is a complex modality of practice and the clinical material and flow of the session throw up many questions. Post-session reflection is a critical part of processing the work to date and shaping its course.

In the case of Rio just mentioned, the therapist found that for a number of sessions after the one described she was unable to broach the events of that day in a meaningful way with the mother. She was puzzled, as she was usually quite able to talk with parents about both ambivalence and hatred. After much self-examination she realized that some of the struggle to discuss the outburst with the mother was linked to shame at having witnessed, and thereby felt she had colluded with, the mother's violence. Probing further, she thought about her shame and also about her helplessness in the moment, that in the initial feeling of shock she did not know how to help them and to protect the baby. This process of self-reflection enabled the therapist, some weeks later, to start talking with mother and baby about what had happened and how it felt.

Supervision is also seen to be a requirement for good practice. Supervision offers a mentalizing perspective on one's practice, particularly as each of us has blind-spots, which we cannot necessarily identify without someone else's thinking. A much-repeated mantra in mentalizing is that it is interactive and that we are dependent on other people's mentalizing to help maintain our own. A therapist may need the help of supervision to restore mentalizing in situations where a case brings particular assaults on the therapist's capacity to think, as described.

References

Avdi, E., & Seikkula, J. (2019). Studying the process of psychoanalytic psychotherapy: Discursive and embodied aspects. *British Journal of Psychotherapy, 35*(2), 217–232. doi:10.1111/bjp.12444

Baradon, T., Biseo, M., Broughton, C., James, J., & Joyce, A. (2016). *The practice of psychoanalytic parent-infant psychotherapy: Claiming the baby* (2nd ed.). London: Routledge.

Cramer, B. (1998). Mother-infant psychotherapies: A widening scope in technique. *Infant Mental Health Journal, 19*(2). doi:10.1002/%28SICI%291097-0355%2819982 2%2919:2%3C151::AID- IMHJ5%3E3.0.CO;2-R

Fraiberg, S., Adelson, E., & Shapiro, V. (1975). Ghosts in the nursery. A psychoanalytic approach to the problems of impaired infant-mother relationships. *Journal of the American Academy of Child Psychiatry, 14*(3), 387–421.

Ransley, R., Sleed, M., Baradon, T., & Fonagy, P. (2019). "What support would you find helpful?" The relationship between treatment expectations, therapeutic engagement, and clinical outcomes in parent–infant psychotherapy. *Infant Mental Health Journal, 40*(4), 557–572. doi:10.1002/imhj.21787

Salomonsson, B., & Sandell, R. (2011a). A randomized controlled trial of mother–infant psychoanalytic treatment: I. Outcomes on self-report questionnaires and external ratings. *Infant Mental Health Journal, 32*(2), 207–231. doi:10.1002/imhj.20291

Salomonsson, B., & Sandell, R. (2011b). A randomized controlled trial of mother–infant psychoanalytic treatment: II. Predictive and moderating influences of qualitative patient factors. *Infant Mental Health Journal, 32*(3), 377–404. doi:10.1002/imhj.20302

Stern, D. N. (1985). *The interpersonal world of the infant: A view from psychoanalysis and developmental psychology*. New York, NY: Basic Books.

Tuckett, D. (2019). Transference and transference interpretation revisited: Why a parsimonious model of practice may be useful. *International Journal of Psychoanalysis, 100*(5), 852–876. doi:10.1080/00207578.2019.1664906

7 Microanalysis of a PPIP case

In this chapter we will illustrate the ideas that we have covered previously by describing material from a PPIP session, with a mentalization perspective added as commentary. The chapter is adapted from previously published papers (Baradon, 2018; Avdi et al., 2020) and represents the work of a small research group at the AFC that is studying clinical process at the micro-level of moment-to-moment interactions between parent, infant and therapist. The group has adopted the multimodal microanalytic approach, as developed by Stern, Beebe, Lachmann, Jaffe and colleagues (Beebe & Lachmann, 2014), and applied it to the therapeutic process itself. Microanalysis enables the examination of the instant-by-instant, temporal-spatial-affective contours of an interactive event: it allows us to see the minutiae of what is happening in the process of therapy – those barely perceptible "grains of sand" referenced by Stern ((Stern, 2010), see Chapter 2) on which relationships are built and can shift. It both provides insight to the live embodied activity in the moment and helps delineate relational patterns: "One can often see the larger panorama of someone's past and current life in the small behaviours and mental acts making up this micro-world" (Stern, 2004, p. xiv).

While the method of microanalysis has been at the forefront of research into parent-infant relationships, its application to clinical material is relatively limited. Beebe has written about two parent-infant therapy cases: in the first, videotaped interactions informed the intervention, and in the second, knowledge of mother-infant microanalysis research informed the treatment (Beebe, 2005). Harrison and Tronick used descriptions of videotaped sequences from the first session in the analysis of a five-year-old boy to illustrate the way multiple and concurrent meaning-making processes occur in dyadic communication (Harrison & Tronick, 2011), while Houghton and Beebe have used video microanalysis in relation to dance/movement therapy (Houghton & Beebe, 2016). Additionally, in our work at the AFC, the analysis of the videoed sessional material includes a focus on the therapist in the matrix of interactions, particularly around rupture and repair.

DOI: 10.4324/9781003024323-7

There is a rich literature on rupture and repair in psychotherapy – those moments where the "working alliance" between therapist and patient is strained, and the significance of their repair for the ongoing success of treatment (Safran, Muran, & Eubanks-Carter, 2011). The research at the AFC draws upon Tronick and colleagues' work on interactive errors and repair in relation to PPIP. As discussed in Chapter 2, mismatches in interaction between parent and infant are common occurrences; they enable a relationship to develop robustness and richness. A perfectly attuned pair would indicate a relationship that is overly cautious and overly protective in character, in which there is insufficient accounting for the separateness of selves. In the microanalysis of therapeutic process, distinction is made between the interactive errors and repair that occur almost automatically and outside of full awareness between parent and infant and therapist, and between interactive ruptures that involve the therapist. Ruptures require reflective work on the part of the therapist: awareness, embodied regulation and mentalization – in order to proceed to repair. Microanalysis allows us to identify the nature of mismatches between infant, parent and therapist, so we can understand their meaning – is this an ordinary, everyday mismatch, or is this a more serious rupture, in which someone's needs are being more powerfully misunderstood or mischaracterized? In effect, it allows us to recognize the more intense and impactful misattunements in the clinical process in order to allow us to work with them and consider their role in the PPIP process. From a mentalizing perspective, we could say that microanalysis allows us to apply reflective mentalizing to a process that is normally automatic. It allows us, for example, to identify the moment where a therapist – often in response to a dysregulating experience with parent or infant – finds him or herself veering towards one of the non-mentalizing modes (see Chapter 5). This may manifest as the therapist feeling that he or she needs to do something (teleological mode), or confusing his/her affect with the infant's or parent's (psychic equivalence), or developing an over-elaborate, inauthentic explanation of what is going on in the room, perhaps to avoid a more confronting emotional reality (pretend mode). As we shall see later, both the complex triangle of parent, baby and therapist minds and the intensity and opacity of infantile experience can generate particularly challenging mentalizing systems within the PPIP consulting room, in which the therapist will inevitably find such modes of thinking emerging. The task for the therapist is to recognize such moments and to bring back online a more balanced form of mentalizing: microanalysis can help the therapist retrospectively recognize and tune into such moments, and thus learn from experience.

The case described here draws on clinical sources – clinical notes written at the time of the therapy and the therapist's reconstruction when viewing the video with the research team, and applies a range of attachment-based measures to the same selected clinical material. The clinical and research measures are integrated in Layered Analysis: this entailed repeatedly reviewing the embodied and verbal exchanges over time in a therapeutic "micro-event", to create an appropriately multi-faceted understanding of interactions. The Layered Analysis is applied in this chapter to material from one particular parent-infant psychotherapy case.

Clinical material

Mother, Joanna, was aged 23 and grew up in an abusive family in Eastern Europe. From the Adult Attachment Interview, conducted early in the PPIP therapy, it became apparent that as a child she lived in constant fear of losing her own mother to drugs and alcohol, and spent extended periods "bringing herself up". Immigration to the UK, a long period of counselling and a satisfying marriage had brought stability to her life. Furthermore, the father of the baby came from a large, stable family who offered ongoing support, and the couple's relationship was close. The pregnancy was planned.

The birth was approached with anticipation but became highly traumatic in that the baby nearly died during labour; there was a danger that if she did survive, there could be extensive brain damage. During her birth and early weeks postnatally, the baby's minute-by-minute experience was saturated with medical interventions and the intrusion of her parents' and professionals' anxiety. The referral for parent-infant psychotherapy came because the mother felt she was not bonding with her baby, Mia, and that Mia "did not like her". The Health Visitor observed that the baby was strikingly avoidant of eye contact and was concerned.

As discussed in Chapter 5, it is harder to think reflectively about mental states when one's attachment needs are on high alert. The frightening birth had probably hyperactivated both Joanna's and Mia's attachment and stress systems, for very understandable reasons. Joanna, who had done considerable psychological work as an adult to think through her earlier experiences and achieve stable and supportive relationships, may have been "knocked back" into some forms of non-mentalizing by the experience of a difficult birth and the demands of earliest motherhood. She was not, it seemed, yet fully able to think about and join with Mia's mental states, and as a result, Mia seemed to be less motivated to engage in face-to-face exchanges with her mother that would normally be expected of a baby of her age. This created something of a vicious cycle, as both mother and infant were unable to join in rewarding experiences of sharing emotional states of mind with one another.

Clinical segment one: extracts from the therapist's notes from the first session

I met with Joanna and Mia when Mia was 6 weeks old, really tiny. Father chose not to attend. I introduced myself to them. Despite approaching her gently and with openness and interest, Mia was very avoidant with me. She was also remarkably serious, and had a blank facial expression. Her posture was somewhat stiff – for example, she did not mould into her mother's body. And yet, Mia was also very "present" in the session with frequent grunts, frets, murmurs. They seemed like noises that expressed a lack of containment rather than intentional communications with expectations of interaction; Joanna responded to the vocalisations by changing Mia's position, without words. It seemed that Joanna, too, did not experience her baby's vocalisations as calls to interact. My sense is that an inhibition of affect is already present in Mia since there seems a limited range of emotions expressed, and the feelings that cannot be held back leak out in the vocalizations. She also did not explore much.

Joanna spoke about the reasons why she has sought help. Since the birth she has felt that while she has sort of bonded Mia, Mia has not bonded with her. For example, Mia wants to be held all the time but does not care who holds her. Mother feels she looks at Mia with a cloud of worry hanging over them. She also has concerns that her baby does not make eye contact with her. The doctors were worried about Mia's eyes as she does not track or make eye contact, but now say that they think her overall development is OK, just lagging.

While talking about these painful matters, Joanna presented a message of "don't probe" in relation to her upset. I wondered whether this is a response to the situation feeling overwhelmingly painful (perhaps frustrating, too), to just meeting me – a stranger – or is it a habitual way of functioning since she was a parentified child?

Watching Mia on her mother's lap over the course of the session, there was little direct interaction. Joanna has a way of peering at Mia's face by looming in from the side; this has the quality of "staring at" rather than seeing, and Mia's unremittingly sober facial expression make it even more difficult to read her cues. The stiffness with which she held herself, and the quality of her vocalisations made me wonder whether Mia held in her body knowledge of her near-death and that this body experience was shaping the nascent prism of her object relationships. Perhaps she avoided me with an embodied memory, an early transference (Salomonsson, 2013), to a dangerous, intrusive object like the medical "strangers" at the hospital?

I commented to Joanna on Mia avoiding my gaze. Joanna said: "she always looks to the side. I don't feel I am getting very much back from her for all the hard work". She sounded brittle, but also immensely sad. Mia's gaze aversion is reinforcing feelings of inadequacy. Are these transgenerational ghosts breaking down the adjustments she has made (through counselling and marriage) so that there is a collapse of present into past?

Looking back at the notes, the therapist noticed how quickly and unusually intense her emotional response to this mother and infant was. There was a concern that the infant could choose an increasingly withdrawn and "switched-off" route for the future, and from this first session the therapist actively involved herself as the baby's therapist alongside the relationship work. As indicated by her engagement with a useful process of counselling, Joanna was in many ways an effective mentalizer – despite her wary and guarded demeanour, she recognized that she needed help with Mia and how she was relating to her. But we can also detect areas where her mentalizing in relation to her baby daughter was somewhat collapsed – the assumption that Mia did not like her (attributing a mental state to Mia that was inaccurate, both on an emotional level and in terms of Mia's capacity to think), and the awkward body language and handling of Mia at times, seemed to indicate that she was not entirely able to either cognitively or bodily mentalize her daughter in a way that fully recognized her developmental stage and needs.

Clinical segment two (session 2; Mia is 9 weeks old)

Joanna settled with Mia on her knee. Mia, grunting and murmuring throughout the session, was moved around from one position to another – sometimes perched on the end of mother's knee facing the therapist, sometimes with her back against her mother, close to her but still facing the therapist. Again, the therapist noticed that the mother would loom in from the side rather than turning her infant to face her.

Within the first few minutes of the session, Joanna and Mia settled on the floor, and Joanna then lifted her face expectantly to the therapist. We report here the transcript of this session.

Transcript from video

THERAPIST (TH) TO JOANNA (J): How's the last week been for you? [Therapist responding to J's look in a warm voice]

Mia looks animated, she is facing therapist and leaning towards her
J says: I can't think, it's gone quick. I felt much better after coming, I
didn't realize how much I needed to talk to somebody, (to) who(m)
I didn't have to say: "but she's all OK now", so it's been quite good.

J leans towards Mia and opens her mouth in a silent "ah". She
rocks Mia, supporting her head. Mia is looking to the distance
beyond her mother.

J continues to talk to the therapist: She's had a bit of a cold so I
didn't want to go out the last three days and I went through two days
of trying to get her to sleep not in my arms, which was just a night-
mare, and I feel like she's upset with me . . .

J giggles slightly and shrugs her shoulders, looking down at Mia
and then at the floor.

Th leans forward, looking thoughtful. She addresses Joanna but
is also looking at Mia, as though inviting her to also tell her story:
Mmm?

J elaborates, her body is open despite the difficulty she describes:
So we had two not very nice days. We had one very good day,
when my mum was there as well, she was really lovely, and then two
grumpy days. Exhausting days with me just taking her out, putting
her in, so she didn't sleep all day! Then, today it has been nice.

Th looks at both with an enquiring face. She asks: So taking her
out of a Moses basket . . .??

J: Yeah, she doesn't like it at all.

Th leans forward to Mia, she shakes her head (giving an ostensive
cue), and talks in motherese: Tell us about that. Mmm? Is it that you
like mummy's skin, and the sme-l-l, and that softness? [Her voice
drops.] Or is it that the Moses basket reminds you of being by yourself in an incubator? [Therapist is modelling her attempts to mentalize Mia, while, in her curious and questioning tone, maintaining the
idea that she cannot know for certain what Mia's mental state is.]

Mia is restless, vocalizing throughout. Joanna's attention seems
with the therapist's speech and Mia reaction

TH (straightens her position and asks Joanna, in an adult voice): And even
when you sit right next to the basket and talk to her?

J is engaged, explaining: She stayed maybe for 10 minutes, she
must have been exhausted, with me singing to her, that seemed to
help, but that will only work once. Normally, even if I put my hand
on her, it doesn't settle her at all, she needs me, completely, to pick
her up, and at the very end of the day, she slept in there for half an
hour, but that was because she hadn't slept the whole day and she
was . . .

While her mother is talking Mia frets and Joanna repositions her on her lap, facing out. Mia looks around quietly.

J continues to talk to the therapist, describing the event: And then I just gave up cos I thought I'll try in a month or something maybe. Because she seemed so unhappy afterwards! [She sounds uncertain.] All day [her voice emphasises the length of time]. So if I tried in the morning, six hours later, she'd still seem unhappy.

J looks intently at the therapist, asking her: I don't know if that's possible?

TH replies in motherese, to Mia: That sounds like a l o n g memory.

J: Exactly! Can she remember that? I don't know, maybe it's just me putting . . . maybe she would have been grumpy that day anyway. [Again she sounds uncertain.]

TH leans back, she takes a moment as though formulating her thoughts, then talks in an adult voice to mother: But you know I think we really don't know about the residue in her body . . . [her voice trails off]

J nods.

TH stretches her legs, as though an unconscious ostensive cue to mother, and continues: Not in the mental memory, but in her body, a kind of feeling of no-comfort from that early period.

J (hesitant): That's true.

J looks at Mia with a smile and says gently to her: Yeah.

TH looks animated as she speaks to baby, in motherese: There might be something that just . . . that just doesn't feel safe. Doesn't feel right for your teeny self (she looks at Mia with raised eyebrows, questioningly).

TH: (to J, in adult voice) I might also be attributing things, I don't know.
TH nods her head

J (aroused and curious): And I was saying to my mum, maybe she'd always have been a kind of baby that doesn't like to be put down.

J is holding Mia's hand, with Mia clasping her finger.

TH (in a collaborative voice to mother): Maybe we can, you know, what we need to do, over time, is help you think of ways to help her settle.

J (with relief, her body relaxes): That would be amazing [Enthusiastic] cos it's a bit ridiculous at the moment . . . I don't really mind rocking her all day, it's a bit disruptive . . . [J half smiles, and shrugs.]

The therapist's reconstruction

The description of the trials and tribulations that passed between mother and baby sounded resonant of a much younger baby. I wondered about Mia's extreme sensitivity to being placed in her Moses basket – at four months, even when slightly ill. I again considered that this infant carried an anxious body memory from her earliest trauma at birth and in Special Care Baby Unit, and that perhaps being placed in the Moses basket re-triggered panicked states around pain and abandonment. Her crying and screaming may have been her way of conveying this experience, yet for her mother this acted as a mnemonic, embodying "ghosts" of her own unthinkable anxieties from childhood. I surmised that the threat of losing Mia called up the panic, helplessness, rage and guilt of her childhood when she had experienced trying and failing, through the fact of being a child, to keep her mother alive. It seemed that these unthinkable anxieties (Winnicott, 1962) were transmitted to Baby in the ordinary handling and holding of the early period which, as observed in the session, were abrupt and silent, and did not feel containing. I was convinced that Mia and Joanna had moved from a physical to a psychological life-and-death situation in which each was re-presenting the other's trauma.

The therapist concluded:

No doubt my feelings and thinking infiltrated my way-of-being in the sessions – I imagine that Mother and Baby felt something of the intensity through the quality of my attention, my facial expressions, and the overall kinaesthetic of my body. I was conscious of the work I needed to do within myself to temper my state of urgency, especially in light of their sensitivity to re-traumatization by worried and intrusive others. I therefore tried to establish a slowed pace in the room, attuned as closely as possible to Baby's rhythms of vocalizations, movement, changes in expression or attention.

In this reconstruction, the therapist explicates the dynamic hypotheses she developed as the clinical material unfolded. She points to the ways in which she processed the upsetting report of a baby who seemingly has not yet recovered from her near-death experience at birth, and a mother who understandably failed to find ways to console her baby. She holds in mind that Joanna may be feeling not only frightened but also heightened ambivalence and, consequently, guilt and shame at her hostile feelings, accentuated by the reawakened ghosts from her nursery. The therapist's countertransference was intensified, and she was aware of this and leads us, the readers of her account, to the psychological-reflective work she needed to do within herself. From a mentalizing perspective, if the therapist had not been able to mentalize herself at this moment, it is possible that one of the non-mentalizing modes of functioning would have coming to the fore, in which the therapist's urgency to act or urgency of feeling would have become too present. We can also notice that the therapist was using the mentalizing stance – suggesting thoughts in an inquiring, tentative and

open way – both in relation to Mia's mental state ("I might also be attributing things, I don't know") and in relation to what Joanna might need from
the therapist ("Maybe we can, you know, what we need to do, over time,
is help you think of ways how to help her settle"). Through this stance, the
therapist was modelling her attempt to mentalize Mia, and also responding
to the difficult time that Joanna had been having with Mia. She did this in
a way that was not catastrophizing or shaming (resisting the urge to "do"
something now for Joanna, in a teleological mode) but recognizing and
validating of Joanna's difficulties and need for help.

Clinical segment three (session 6; Mia is aged 20 weeks)

This session took place the week after the therapist had conducted the
AAI with Joanna; in the interview her disturbing childhood experiences
had been described in a coherent, thoughtful way. The session started
with a focus on Mia.

Transcript from video

As they settled on the mat Joanna propped baby Mia up and spoke to her.

JOANNA (to Mia): Do you remember it here? Mmm, all these bright
    things to look at.
        She placed Mia in a sitting position on the floor leaning on a
    cushion and then sat down next to her. They were both facing the
    therapist.
        Mia is looking to the distance and vocalizes, Joanna looks down
    at her
        Therapist tilts her head to the left, and curves her body slightly[1]
THERAPIST (to baby in motherese): We've learnt to wait, haven't we
    Mia? . . . Till you are ready to look . . .
        There is a brief pause. The therapist is looking at Mia and Joanna
    is sitting by her, watching.
TH: And sometimes it takes a little bit of time. Mmm?
        Th smiles at Mia, nods her head, eyebrows raised, and continues,
    slowly and in sing-song, as baby now raises her eyes and looks at the
    therapist.
TH nods her head once as she speaks: "Now you are ready".
        Joanna leans in from the side to see Mia's face
        Th continues to speak to baby, nodding her head in time: But you
    like to take things in first, don't you? Mm?
TH continues *to vocalize:* "*y- e-s . . . mmm*" *while baby engages visually with*
    her.

Discourse analysis

The therapist addresses the baby but positions herself together with Joanna ("we") as having learnt to adapt to Mia's need to pace her herself, to self-regulate within the interaction (i.e., waiting for Mia to be ready to look). In this way, Mia's behaviour is represented as respected, and therapist and Joanna are positioned together as adults who adapt to her, but who have needed time to learn to do this appropriately.

The therapist then talks to Mia about her inner state. In her talk, the therapist positions Mia as a person who needs her time before looking – this reconstructs Mia's gaze aversion from a possible symptom into a meaningful action on her part; she is also positioned as someone who is attentive (i.e., in touch with her environment) and possibly careful/cautious – someone who likes (rather than needs) to take things in first.

In this turn, several therapeutic functions seem to be taking place: Mia is positioned as a participant in the dialogue in her own right – on a verbal level, she is addressed as an equal interactional partner whose interactional preferences are taken into account and respected. On a non-verbal level, the therapist seems keen to engage Mia in an interaction, to draw her out, and she does this respectfully in relation to Mia's interactional style; she speaks to her in a gentle tone, looks at her attentively and mirrors her facial expression (pout). She marks (and responds to) Mia turning her gaze to her with a warm smile and describes Mia's engagement in the interaction verbally too ("now you're ready"). In this way, the therapist's verbal and non-verbal communications are congruent and could be described as communicating something along the lines of "I would like to engage with you, at your own pace and on your own terms". The therapist's behaviours could be read as ostensive cues, priming Mia to understand that this might be a fruitful interaction, in which it is pleasurable and interesting to share attention. The quality of the exchange suggests that at this point in the session, the therapist and Mia have started to establish a way of being with each other in which Mia is able to help shape the levels of engagement. This brief attuned encounter was disrupted by the following interaction.

Clinical segment four: microanalysis of 5 seconds

Mia had been gazing steadily at the therapist for 12 seconds as the therapist spoke, and then paused.

Mia lowered her gaze and turned her head towards the window – 45 degrees.

Therapist glances at the direction of Mia's gaze and then continues to look at Mia, her body relaxed and open.

Joanna sees Mia turn away, and gives a shrieking-like laugh. She turns to face the therapist with a "smile" still on her face while, at the same time, leaning away from her (invites sharing but contradicts it by withdrawing).

Therapist faces Joanna with a bewildered look and questioning smile.

Joanna turns away from therapist to Mia.

Joanna says "Oh dear . . ." in a lingering, whispering tone and touches Baby's averted head lightly. She looks disoriented.

Therapist glances at mother.

Joanna's body settles, Joanna and therapist return their gaze to Mia, who is still looking in the direction of the window

In this sequence, Joanna responds to Mia breaking eye contact with the therapist in a way that marks it as psychologically/emotionally problematic to her. Her response (the strained laughter and grimaced smile) is incongruent both with the initial mentalizing of the Mia (Do you remember?) and with the interactive rhythm that the therapist and Mia have started to establish between them, and cuts across it. The rapidly changing, fleeting and subtle facial expressions and tones of voice in Joanna indicate that she is in a highly frightened and disoriented state of mind, as seen by the large number of anomalous behaviours in this brief moment. These behaviours are likely to be frightening to the baby. At the same time, the therapist freezes and seems thrown off kilter, briefly mirroring the mother's disoriented state of mind, before she repositions herself physically and addresses Joanna.

Therapist's reconstruction

My clinical notes written after the session documented the confusion and unease I felt in response to Joanna's laugh and the difficulty I had coming back into the interactions. At the time, when Mia turned away, I was confident that she was regulating her intense emotional response to our engagement, which I had experienced as a shared state in which I, too, was highly involved and pleased that Mia was coming out of her avoidance. I expected that she would turn back to me when ready and thus cue her interest in resuming our proto-conversation. I was relaxed but alert as I waited. I felt confident that we were in the midst of an attuned exchange and more would come. Joanna's "laugh" cut across this expectancy. It was rapid and high pitched and felt quite contrary to the slow musical rhythm established in the exchange with Mia. Not only did it take me completely by surprise, but I felt disrupted in my own experience of myself, and my shared experience with the baby. Similarly, her utterance "O dear" was confusing – it was unclear as to whom she was addressing: me, Mia, herself, or the situation. The impact was highly dysregulating and I could not think clearly. Unsure of how to respond, I tried to hide behind what I hoped was an enquiring smile as I turned to Joanna to ascertain what had happened.

The therapist clearly describes here how her capacity to mentalize was shut down in the moment of heightened negative emotion associated disruption.

Therapist's commentary

On watching the video in the research forum – tracking, frame by frame, the unfolding of movements towards and away from each other – constituted an "aha" moment for me as the therapist. My first realisation was the extent to which disruption of benign attachment expectancies, in this case the expectancy to resume calm interaction with Mia, does indeed violate one's sense of knowing oneself and sense of safety with the other. I felt I could understand why such experiences, when regular occurrences, disorganize an infant's self-experience and attachment manoeuvres. The second insight was into the immediacy, intensity and "truthfulness" of embodied communication: my inner state of disorganization was expressed in freezing and grimacing (the little "enquiring smile" I thought I had assumed). These were subtle and fleeting facial expressions but sufficiently potent in conveying to mother and baby my own disoriented state of mind. This momentary mutual arousal between baby, mother and myself triggered a further disrupted behaviour as mother turned to her baby in the beginning of an intrusive loom. By that point, I was sufficiently reorganized in myself to interrupt the loom, and break the in-the-moment spiral of traumatization.

Clinical segment 5 (later in the same session)

The session continued and after a while the conversation came back to Joanna's experience of the AAI. Joanna spoke about her disappointment that the past has come alive after so many years of counselling. As these upsetting feelings surfaced, Mia became unsettled. She was lying on her back between us and her fretting turned into cries. Her legs and arms were flailing. The therapist's attention shifted to her and she took a conscious decision to address Mia's own trauma with her, and the links with Joanna's experiences.

Transcript from video with clinical and mentalizing commentaries

THERAPIST (TH) vocalizes "mmm, yes?" as she slowly leans in and brings her face nearer and Mia gazes at her.

Th strokes Mia rhythmically on her chest and stomach.

TH: Are you telling us something? Are you telling us? [Voice rises in question]

Mia slows down her movements, and looks into Th's face. She maintains a steady gaze. Joanna, crouching next to Mia, strokes her foot and watches her in interaction with Th.

[In posing the question: are you telling us something? The therapist again positions Mia as agent and transform her cries into intentional communication. "Us" places mother and therapist as a reflective parenting couple who is committed to understanding the infant – mentalizing minds who can privilege Mia's experience.]

TH: That you are a sen-si-tive [sing-song voice] little thing, sensitive to what's going on, aren't you . . .?

[The therapist is preparing the ground for further exploration of Mia's anxieties: she is both a sensitive being in herself, and a person aware of emotional currents surrounding her. The therapist is therein presenting multiple perspectives in considering Mia and reframing mother's perception of avoidance as an expression of lack of love for her and the representation of the baby as unloving.]

There is a brief pause, the therapist continues stroking the Mia's chest and stomach with even movements and Joanna again lightly touches her foot

[The pause is significant. It provides time for the three participants in the interaction to steady themselves within the emotional vortex of revisiting the birth trauma.]

TH [using same tone of voice and intonations]: And not only did you have your o w n anxieties, when you were being born, yeah and you had to s u r v i v e but you know your mummy and daddy were so worried . . .

[The therapist reinforces the view of the baby as sentient – able to apprehend emotions in her close environment.]

Mia looks at her mother and her mother nods

[This is the first formulation in the therapy that is directed to the baby about her life-death predicament. But the therapist refers not only to Mia the baby but also to the parents and infant as a unit during those moments of trauma. In this way, mother and baby can share that experience in the present moment.]

TH: Now e v e r y b o d y is trying to be confident.

[This last sentence is spoken in a somewhat forced way and the timbre of the therapist voice is louder and harsher than before. Her words introduce a foreign element to the fluidity of the therapist's previous formulations: "trying to be confident" suggests a conscious effort rather than confidence built on experience of the baby's survival and progress. Speaking of "confidence" in the baby's development further raises the question of "will she be alright" (in the future) and suggests, therein, that she perhaps is not alright now.]

Mia vocalizes, seeming to choke a little. Th stops talking and stops her stroking, looking concerned. Joanna also stills momentarily.

Mia chokes at this moment.

[Of course, there is room for co-incidence. But in line with the thinking above, it may have been in response to the change in the therapist.]

Both Joanna and therapist respond with concern to the split-second interaction.

TH: Oh? What's going on? Did you get a lot of saliva in your mouth? . . . (pause)

Or (lowered voice) was that a b i g idea to have to digest. Yeah, it i-s, i-s-n't it? How f r a g i l e you were".

[The therapist attributes psychological meaning to the cough while also acknowledging a purely physical explanation. But she (therapist) does not attribute it to her mixed communication which immediately precedes the "cough". Although aware, as she is saying the sentence, that something feels 'off', the therapist is unable, in the moment, to identify what feels wrong and formulate it as an interactive error. The therapist goes back to her preoccupation with the trauma. But now something seems to have resolved in her as she is able to incorporate Mia's survival without hesitation]:

TH: *"But you s u r v i v ed, y e a h, and you are doing so well"*.

Mia calms.

This confirmation of Mia's progress is spoken in the same undulating motherese that characterised most of the therapist's speech. It repairs the interactive error and restores a shared state between therapist and baby. However, it appears that the repair had not contained mother's negative arousal.

The therapist's clinical notes state:

But just then something – below conscious register – alerted me that I had to support mother. Jolted, I pulled back from Baby to turn to her mother. With a sharp movement Mother massaged her foot saying said she had "pins and needles" and had to stand up to try and shake off the pain. Baby started whimpering again and Mother's trajectory of distress escalated. And then I was out of tune with both.

Therapist's commentary

This interaction was extremely complex. On the one hand, I was trying to address core anxieties I perceived in Mia, through speaking to them in an emotionally resonant way. Verbal and embodied languages were intertwined. I needed words, since words are for me *"pathways into direct embodied experiences* that function implicitly" (Nahum, 2008, p. 133, italics added). My bodily communication was probably most important for Mia to feel genuinely known and contained. Her little choke could be seen to symbolize the psychological work that was taking place (Winnicott, 1972). On the other hand, by putting into words Mia's traumatic experiences I inevitably scratched at Joanna's anxiety and guilt, perhaps thereby becoming a persecuting figure at that moment (Baradon & Bronfman, 2009). Aware of this, perhaps through cues from Joanna that I picked up in my peripheral vision, I purposely tried to balance the death and anxiety end of the scales with Mia's survival and the hope that she is intact. There was a moment of coming together, when Mia turned to look at Joanna and Joanna responded by nodding. At this point I felt that the dialogue between mother and baby was open and inclusive. As Lyon-Ruth states "open dialogue is characterised . . . by parental openness to the state of mind of the child, including the entire array of the child's communication, so that particular affective or motive states of the child (anger, passion, distress) are not foreclosed from intersubjective sharing and regulation" (Lyons-Ruth, 1999, p. 583). However, the sentence I added that *"everyone* is *trying* to be *confident"* seemed to undo this previous sharing. I believe that what unconsciously leaked into this sentence was my uncertainty that Joanna could recognise Mia's healthy potential. At that level, my sentence was disingenuous. I also held criticism of Joanna of which I was unaware in the moment, but it is clear, upon viewing the video, how my embodied communication conveyed this. Cumulatively, Joanna became increasingly dysregulated. The symptom of "pins and needles" was poignant: the needles of her mother's addiction, of the medical interventions to save her baby's life, and the jabs of her own pain.

My experience of the session required considerable reflection and self-examination afterwards. The enactments between Joanna and me illuminated many aspects of the embodied communications about trauma between mother and baby. It also clarified how the transmission of trauma in this dyad was made actual.

The first enactment occurred when Mia turned away to self-regulate after an intense engagement with me. Joanna's eerie laugh seemed to condense relief that she was not alone in being "rejected" and triumph that despite my alignment with Mia it happened to me too. These emotions were underpinned by the sharpness of loss, and feelings of being spurned. The second enactment – that of pins and needles – followed my addressing Mia's life and death experience, shrouded in continuing anxiety. Only after the event was I able to properly reflect on my contributions to Joanna's state. Was I perceived as "successfully" engaging with her daughter, thus increasing feelings of rejection and resentment and adding to her narcissistic wound? I wondered about my urgency to offer experiences of relatedness to Mia. Was her need to be understood resonating an internal state in me? Was I also "nudged" (Sandler, 1976) into responding to a communication from Mia to help her to "take the risks involved in starting to experience living" (Winnicott, 1956), by behaviourally countering environmental impingements. Joanna's response was more conflicted – wanting and not wanting to address the cumulative trauma – and her responsiveness was, as a result, perhaps more confused and less satisfactory to her.

Discussion

The micro- and layered analyses highlight the rapid movement in and out of attuned states between therapist, mother and baby. Attuned, shared states may encompass all three participants or may move between changing dyadic alliances. Interactive errors occur frequently, and remain as fleeting mis-attuned micro-events because of a move to repair. However, at times rapid repair is not possible because the therapist has not been able to process the embodied knowledge ("something is wrong") to symbolic formulation quickly enough. Considerations of the therapist's psychological work towards repair are addressed in Chapter 9.

A hallmark of this case was the shared "anxiety of being" (Durban, 2017). In the mother this state was induced in infancy by her experiences of her mother's absence (through addiction to drugs), and later through conscious fears that her mother would abandon her through death. In turn, Mia was born with a bodily imprint of near-death, which was perpetuated by ongoing intrusive investigations into, and anxieties about, her development. We suggest that such experience induced in her a panic of annihilation, evidenced in her alternating withdrawal and inconsolability. In this way, mother and baby exquisitely mirrored the threat of loss and anxiety-of-(not)-being to each other, and trauma was kept alive for each from without and from within.

In one of her early sessions, Joanna spoke of the years of counselling she had undertaken to process her childhood experiences. She described this therapeutic work as critical in bringing her to the point where she felt she would be able parent a child of her own. One of the questions raised in this case is the role of the birth in reactivating childhood trauma in the mother: had the birth been straightforward would mother and daughter thrived, in the embrace of the nuclear and extended paternal family? Would a PPIP intervention still have been needed by them? Traumatic delivery is recognized as a stressor and trigger for posttraumatic symptomatology post-partum (Ayers, 2004). Numerous studies have also explored how childbirth may retraumatize women who were sexually abused in childhood due to the women's association of the delivery with their earlier maltreatment (Courtois & Courtois, 1992; Daphna-Tekoah, Lev-Wiesel, & Ben-Zion, 2015; Jacobs, 1992). In this instance, the nature of the birth trauma uncannily mirrored Mother's childhood situation and went to the heart of the core anxieties around survival: her own as a young child lacking parental protection, as a child unable (developmentally) to ensure her mother's survival, as a mother to keep her newborn alive. It is not surprising, therefore, that internal processes of reorganization towards a healthy motherhood constellation (Stern, 1995; see Chapter 4) were disrupted, and the primary and organizing representation of motherhood as a failing mother resurfaced. Additionally, Mia – now endowed with the hues of the deficient mother – became a constant reminder of this failure. In a sense, it was not only Mia whose gaze was avoidant – both mother and baby avoided gazing at the other, it was a co-constructed defence (see Chapter 2).

The particular state of mind of shared anxiety was expressed in complex ways across the spectrum of both verbal and embodied communication. For example, Mia's presentation in Segment One indicated that states of mind were both inhibited (blank expression, stiff body) and irrupting (grunts). Similarly, the quality of Joanna's looming held in it a desperate attempt to "see" her baby and, at the same time, an inability to "know" her. Vocalizations and gestures, in particular, seemed to constitute a form of perceptual priming, procedural triggers to threat and hyperarousal for each partner (Ehlers & Clark, 2000).

The therapist's interventions were embodied and verbal. Lieberman and Harris address the responsibility of the therapist in "articulating viscerally rending experiences so that the parent and the child can differentiate between remembering and reliving the trauma and can learn to anticipate and modulate overwhelming responses to the memories" (Lieberman & Harris, 2007). Harrison and Tronick propose that somatic (non-verbal) communications carry dynamic meaning and as such are features of therapeutic action as much as verbal communications: "At any one moment, a slice of communication can be examined that represents what we call a 'polysemic bundle' of communicative behaviours, a bundle that includes a mix of language and somatic expressions of meaning" (Harrison & Tronick, 2011, p. 963). Indeed, it was in addressing the baby-mother trauma that cross-modal embodied communications were most strongly interwoven with the therapist's verbal interventions. Thus, words such as "fragile" (so "fra" – lowered tone – "gile" – head dropped, eyebrows raised) and "survived" ("sur- v-i i i ved" – drawn out intonation, raised pitched, widened eyes) were wrapped, in the moment, in a particular embodied contour to reach out to the previously unthinkable. The AFC Clinical Process research group has concluded that

> In attuned interactions, verbal and embodied modes of communication languages appear to reinforce the meaning of the other: bodily communication non-consciously scaffolds the verbal communication and accentuates the meaning of what is being said. Verbal communication clarifies and amplifies the embodied message. The rhythms overlap and form a specific emotional contour . . . But in non-attuned interactions verbal and embodied communications may conflict, with each mode of communication undermining the message of the other.
>
> (Paper in progress)

The transcriptions of the clinical vignettes illustrate this observed relationship between embodied and verbal communication.

But what of the therapist initiating touch of Mia in response to her states of physical/affective agitation? Traditionally in psychoanalysis this would be viewed as "outside the framework", possibly even breaking the boundaries that protect the baby patient. We suggest that touch, thoughtfully used, can be an inherent property of intervention for young infants. Feldman and colleagues established that maternal touch attenuates the infant's physiological reactivity to stress, particularly after/during moments of maternal absence, withdrawal, deprivation (Feldman, Singer, & Zagoory-Sharon, 2010). Perhaps, when the mother is emotionally and physically unavailable to a dysregulated infant, the therapist may step in with attuned and synchronous touch to down-regulate distress. Furthermore, the authors above state that behavioural markers of stress – fussing, kicking, crying, gaze aversion – were substantially reduced when the research infant was being touched during maternal deprivation. This was the case for Mia, although the touch was not independent of the therapist's reflective talking and overall body kinaesthetic of mentalizing the baby, which Shai and Belsky have termed "embodied mentalizing" (Shai & Belsky, 2011).

Note

1 Conducted by Dr Evrinomy Avdi

References

Avdi, E., Amiran, K., Baradon, T., Broughton, C., Sleed, M., Spencer, R., & Shai, D. (2020). Studying the process of psychoanalytic parent-infant psychotherapy: Embodied and discursive aspects. *Infant Mental Health Journal, 41*(5), 589–602. doi:10.1002/imhj.21888

Avdi, E., & Seikkula, J. (2019). Studying the process of psychoanalytic psychotherapy: Discursive and embodied aspects. *British Journal of Psychotherapy, 35*(2), 217–232. doi:10.1111/bjp.12444

Ayers, S. (2004). Delivery as a traumatic event: Prevalence, risk factors, and treatment for postnatal posttraumatic stress disorder. *Clinical Obstetrics and Gynecology, 47*(3), 552–567. doi:10.1097/01.grf.0000129919.00756.9c

Baradon, T. (2018). Microanalysis of multimodal communication in therapy: A case of relational trauma in parent-infant psychoanalytic psychotherapy. *Journal of Infant, Child, and Adolescent Psychotherapy, 17*(1), 1–13. doi:10.1080/15289168.2017.1415101

Baradon, T., & Bronfman, E. (2009). Contributions of, and divergences between, clinical work and research tools relating to trauma and disorganization. In T. Baradon (Ed.), *Relational trauma in infancy: Psychoanalytic, attachment and neuropsychological contributions to parent infant psychotherapy* (pp. 163–179). London: Routledge.

Beebe, B. (2005). Mother-infant research informs mother-infant treatment. *Psychoanal Study Child, 60*, 7–46. doi:10.1080/00797308.2005.11800745

Beebe, B., & Lachmann, F. M. (2014). *The origins of attachment: Infant research and adult treatment.* New York, NY: Routledge.

Courtois, C. A., & Courtois, R. C. (1992). Pregnancy and childbirth as triggers for abuse memories: Implications for care. *Birth, 19*(4), 222–223.

Daphna-Tekoah, S., Lev-Wiesel, R., & Ben-Zion, I. Z. (2015). Childbirth as retraumatization of childhood sexual abuse. In C. Martin, V. Preedy, & V. Patel (Eds.), *Comprehensive guide to post-traumatic stress disorder* (pp. 1–15). Cham: Springer.

Durban, J. (2017). Home, homelessness and nowhere-ness in early infancy. *Journal of Child Psychotherapy, 43*, 175–191. doi:10.1080/0075417X.2017.1327550

Ehlers, A., & Clark, D. M. (2000). A cognitive model of posttraumatic stress disorder. *Behaviour Research and Therapy, 38*, 319–345.

Feldman, R., Singer, M., & Zagoory-Sharon, O. (2010). Touch attenuates physiological reactivity to stress. *Developmental Science, 13*(2), 271–278.

Harrison, A. M., & Tronick, E. (2011). "The noise monitor": A developmental perspective on verbal and non-verbal meaning maiking in psychoanalysis. *Journal of the American Psychoanalytic Association, 59*(5), 961–982.

Houghton, R., & Beebe, B. (2016). Dance movement therapy: Learning to look through video microanalysis. *American Journal of Dance Therapy, 38,* 334–357. doi:10.1007/s10465-016-9226-0

Jacobs, J. L. (1992). Child sexual abuse victimization and later sequelae during pregnancy and childbirth. *Journal of Child Sexual Abuse, 1*(1), 103–112. doi:10.1300/J070v01n01_07

Lieberman, A. F., & Harris, W. W. (2007). Still searching for the best interests of the child: Trauma treatment in infancy and early childhood. *Psychoanalytic Study of the Child, 62*(1), 211–238. doi:10.1080/00797308.2007.11800790

Lyons-Ruth, K. (1999). The two person unconscious: Intersubjective dialogue, enactive relational representation and the emergence of new forms of relational organisation. *Psychoanalytic Inquiry, 19*(4), 576–617.

Nahum, J. (2008). Forms of relational meaning: Issues in the relations between the implicit and reflective-verbal domains: Boston change process study group. *Psychoanalytic Dialogues, 18*(2), 125–148.

Safran, J. D., Muran, J. C., & Eubanks-Carter, C. (2011). Repairing alliance ruptures. *Psychotherapy, 48*(1), 80–87. doi:10.1037/a0022140

Salomonsson, B. (2013). Transference in parent-infant psychoanalytic treatment. *International Journal of PsychoAnalysis, 94*(4), 767–792.

Sandler, J. (1976). Countertransference and role-responsiveness. *International Review of Psycho-Analysis, 3,* 43–47.

Shai, D., & Belsky, J. (2011). When words just won't do: Introducing parental embodied mentalizing. *Child Development Perspectives, 5*(3), 173–180.

Stern, D. N. (1995). *The motherhood constellation: A unified view of parent-infant psychotherapy.* New York: Basic Books.

Stern, D. N. (2004). *The present moment in psychotherapy and everyday life.* New York: Norton.

Stern, D. N. (2010). *The present moment in psychotherapy and everyday life.* London: W. W. Norton.

Winnicott, D. W. (1956). On transference. *International Journal of Psycho-Analysis, 37*(4–5), 386–388.

Winnicott, D. W. (1962 [1965]). Ego integration in child development. In D. W. Winnicott (Ed.), *The maturational processes and the facilitating environment* (pp. 56–63). London: Hogarth Press.

Winnicott, D. W. (1972). Basis for self in body. *International Journal of Child Psychotherapy, 1,* 7–16.

8   Adapting PPIP for group work in the community

This chapter describes the approach developed over the years to make PPIP accessible by adapting the model and taking it into frontline community settings. Anna Freud did not consider psychoanalysis of children to be exclusively a therapy that takes place in the consulting room. She thought the principles of psychoanalysis could be applied to create environments in which children could learn, overcome adversity and thrive as individuals and within their community. These ideas form the backdrop to further developments in the PPIP model in terms of taking the work to community locations, in situations where coming to a specialist mental health setting might be an obstacle that stops families from receiving help.

When the AFC started offering parent-infant psychotherapy, it transpired that there was a population potentially in-need living just a few doors down the road; an old house had been converted into a hostel for homeless women where a number of mothers and babies resided. As has been shown, the predicament of families in temporary accommodation is that poverty and housing stresses often come on top of prior trauma and mental health issues (Hogg, Haines, Baradon, & Cuthbert, 2015). The AFC reached out to the mothers and babies in the local and surrounding hostels, offering access to PPIP at the Centre. However, we quickly found that those who crossed the centre's threshold rarely stayed in therapy. Depression, hopelessness, fear of being labelled, preoccupation with ongoing trauma such as domestic violence, dealing with asylum claims or rejection by family of origin – all these impinged on the ability to hold on to the therapy. Commonly described as "hard-to-reach" populations, we realized that such labels may not be an accurate description of what was going on for some of these families. Perhaps what the AFC offered was in fact "hard to access"? We urgently needed to develop a more naturalistic model of delivery which would be less structured and imposing for those partaking in it and could be delivered in community locations where parents and babies congregate, such as health-visiting

DOI: 10.4324/9781003024323-8

baby clinics, baby groups in children's centres and also specialized settings such as hostel or prisons.

We previously discussed the characteristics of mentalizing and non-mentalizing social systems and their impact on the parent and infant. The relationship of these ideas about social environments to our clinical practice is crucial because the difficult reality is that many of the families we encounter will be inhabiting social environments that are experienced as non-mentalizing (Fonagy et al., 2021), as can be the case, for example, in hostels. The benefits of bringing help to a community setting such as a hostel are indicated in a study that found

> an unequivocal improvement in the cognitive and motor develop-ment of the infants in the intervention hostel [where a PPIP group was held in tandem with normal baby health care services] relative to those in the control hostels [where health care was provided without the PPIP group] over time.
> (Sleed, James, Baradon, Newbery, & Fonagy, 2013, p. 11)

A community group seeks to create a mentalizing environment tailored to the infants' ages and parental needs. In many instance this is supportive of growth, but in some cases, this can create conflict for a parent and baby when their wider environment actively discourages mentalizing. Such cultural pressures on a family must be accommodated within the group. For example, a mother comes in and says

> my mother-in-law says that if my baby won't eat, I have to hold him down and make him take the food but I heard you say to [another mother in the group] that she should wait until her baby is ready.

A facilitator is cautioned against leaking her own feelings about forced feeding in order to be able to help the mother consider her own feelings in this complicated situation. It also has to be acknowledged that an individu-al's capacity to generalize from the therapeutic input from the group may be limited by a rigidly held belief system or a more powerful non-mentalizing environment (Bateman, Campbell, Luyten, & Fonagy, 2018).

Delivery of PPIP in the community can entail providing dyad/tri-adic therapy as described in the previous chapters, but more frequently involves adapting the model and integrating it into group formats. While the delivery of dyadic-triadic PPIP in a community location requires the preparation of a safe and reliable room within a location that is often busy, changing and noisy – as community hubs often are – the model does not differ from that described in Chapters 4 and 6 and therefore it is not elaborated on here. This chapter will focus instead on the model of the community-based PPIP group intervention.

There are various advantages that community-based groups offer:

- Accessibility – there is growing evidence to show that establishing the provision of early years help in a "neutral", non-stigmatizing local settings can make a real difference in encouraging families to access help and support. Provision in a location where families ordinarily visit can make it much easier for families to attend, without having to overcome fears of stigma or judgement that might be associated with a more specialized mental health setting.
- Supportive environments for parents and baby – the groups provide and model the characteristics of an environment that promotes infant development. In terms of the setting, they offer stability, reliability and predictability. In terms of the ambiance and rhythm of the group, they provide an experience and model of relational attentiveness for the adults while also being baby-led in focus.
- Agency and mutuality. In the group setting, parents learn from each other and from other babies as much as from the facilitators. Being able to help another parent can help parents feel greater confidence in themselves as parents.
- Reduction is social isolation. During the perinatal period, parents can feel particularly isolated and fragile. Connecting with other families can reduce social isolation and feelings of marginalization.
- Reaching babies at risk. Embedding infant mental health in local services and provision in the community enables both preventive work and can provide a means of reaching those at risk at an earlier stage.

Community-based PPIP

In group formats, as in dyadic/triadic parent-infant psychotherapy, the approach is to support positive attachments and social connectedness. For example, a large enough mat is arranged on the floor so that adults and babies can all share the same space, and the therapist is actively engaged in the hub-bub. Toys are placed centrally for the babies to choose from and share. The culture is to link adults and babies with each other as much as is comfortable for each of the participants. Babies may cross the mat to watch or engage with another baby, and sometimes they may form their own little group.

A baby-led culture

In many traditional clinics or baby groups, the focus is implicitly on the adults – their state of mind and their communications about themselves and their babies. In PPIP-led groups, babies are "centres of attention" and of equal interest as their parents. They are noticed, engaged, wondered about, spoken to and played with. All interactions are directed to enhance their agency and communication abilities, and to highlight to their parents the notion that babies are sentient.

The following illustration has been extracted from videos taken for the evaluation of a children's centre before and after reconfiguration from an educational baby group to a PPIP baby group:

> The pre-reconfiguration video of the baby drop-in showed eight baby mats, each occupied by a mother and older-infant dyad. Small piles of brightly coloured educational toys were placed beside each dyad, selected by the mothers for play with their babies during the group. The facilitator stood on the side and watched. When she noticed a dyad "at a loss" with each other she approached them, crouching down to talk to the mother and/or demonstrate how to engage the baby with a toy. The room was silent but for the lowered voices of the adults and occasional babbling or crying babies.
>
> After changing into a PPIP group the room was set up with one large mat and with various toys in the centre. Mothers and babies were invited to sit on the mat. Little groups formed and then changed around as mothers and facilitators joined each other in informal conversations. The very young babies (absent from the pre-change group, which only attracted mothers with older babies) were attended to by their mothers, but crawling babies moved around exploring other babies and maternal laps. The room was buzzy but relaxed.
>
> (AFC, unpublished report)

An evaluation was conducted comparing the original educationally oriented format of the control group with the reconfigured PPIP intervention group. The evaluation showed substantially more infant-focused, sensitive and cohesive interactions between the adults and babies in the intervention group.

The group as an attachment object

Establishing trust and safety, particularly within a drop-in group where members may vary from week to week, can be a challenge. Individuals come to groups with many different needs. High amongst them is the need to feel included. People inevitably enter a group situation concerned about how they will fit in, wondering if they will like the other people, and/or feel liked by them. A pivotal contribution to building trust is made by the idea of the group itself as an attachment object (James, 2016). In a community of parents and babies, the group "becomes an attachment object when it's experienced by parents and babies as a secure setting that offers a sense of belonging and acceptance" (James, 2016, p. 147). It comes to represent a stable and reliable presence that is interested in the wellbeing and development of the babies and their parents. This was illustrated, in extremis, by the facilitators of one newly formed PPIP group, who sat week after week for the full duration of the group, without any attendees. Although deeply discouraged, they were held by their supervisor's conviction that in time parents and babies would become curious and venture in. Indeed, after nearly six weeks, small forays were made by some parents. Soon suspiciousness was allayed by word-of-mouth recommendations that it was a "decent place" and the group developed to become a steady and well-used local feature of the very deprived community.

The group element is also of crucial importance for the babies. On the one hand, a "baby group" often forms as the infants explore, become interested in what another baby or parent is up to and respond to one another and their approaches. On the other hand, observing and thinking about the baby congregation

> can foster greater awareness in the mothers of the babies' responses to their actions, evoking surprise, pride and pleasure. Mothers can visibly take on aspects of attuned and sensitive care demonstrated by other members of the group and/or modelled by facilitators.
>
> (Baradon et al., 2017)

Observation, reflective listening and curiosity

A sense of safety within the group is enhanced by the facilitators modelling a stance of non-judgemental observation, reflective listening and curiosity. An observation of an ordinary sequence between parent and baby can be used to engage the whole group in thinking about the meaning of what has just happened for the dyad and each partner in it, and to be meaningful to others in the group.

> An example from a PPIP group in a children's centre:
> A baby rolled away from her mother and found herself close to another mother (mother 2). She grabbed hold of the other mother's shirt and pulled it into her mouth. Glancing up towards that mother's face, she looked shocked and started crying when she realised she was not with her own mother. The facilitator said: "Oh, what happened? Did you expect to see mummy's face?" Mother 2 smiled at the baby and gently stroked her saying "oh dear, oh dear".

The facilitator turned to the baby's mother: "Maybe she suddenly realised she was separated from you and got a fright?". The mother looked embarrassed. A third mother (mother 3), who had noticed this event, commented reassuringly: "she (baby) looks alright now" and, indeed, the baby had calmed. A short exchange between the mothers followed:

MOTHER 3: She was fine, it's good for them (babies) to learn new faces

MOTHER 2: Yea, but still, I like to keep her close (referring to her own baby)

MOTHER 1: I don't know . . . what is good for the baby? It's different from what my husband and his family say, they say I should be doing things differently.

FACILITATOR: What is good for a baby? That is such an important question. And we have so many ideas right here in the group.

The vignette illustrates how, when group members can hold on to an observing and reflecting position, the group can feel safe enough for different views to be expressed. These differing perspectives offer a mentalizing environment about the babies. Moreover, the parents' experiences of being understood themselves can translate into greater awareness of their babies' psychological experiences. In parallel, the facilitators' direct work with the babies, in which they consider the babies' communications about how they are feeling, serve to make the infants' mental states more accessible to their parents. For example, the most frequent feedback from participants in many groups has been "I understand my baby better" and "I realize that s/he has his/her own feelings from the beginning".

Grabbing the moment

"Grabbing the moment" (James & Rosan, 2019) was a description used by a health visitor to describe the importance of the facilitator's attention and responses to what is happening between a mother and her baby in the group at that instant. In drop-in groups, the rationale for grabbing the moment is particularly strong because families come and go and staff do not know if and when there may be another opportunity to intervene, so responses have to be made in the moment. However, although central to the culture of the drop-in group, the idea of capitalizing on the here-and-now to speak to both the particular mother-infant dyad and the group as a whole is a feature of structured groups as well. The following is an example of such an intervention with a mother and her eight-month baby boy attending a drop-in group for the first time:

> A mother came in and sat at the fringes of the group. The facilitator greeted her and the baby and helped them settle. A little later she noticed the baby looking with interest at other babies playing, but he seemed held back tightly by his mother who still looked awkwardly shy. "Mummy", the facilitator said, speaking for the baby, "can I go and explore? Will you be alright if I leave you briefly?" then in her adult voice the facilitator added "the first time in a group can be hard, we see that with all first-timers, can you tell me about you and baby" and settled with mother. A few minutes later another mother and her young baby were invited to join the conversation.

This intervention illustrates a multilayered intervention taking place in such a grabbed moment. It addressed the age-appropriate developmental need of the baby to discover his surroundings within the safe orbit of mother and group ("can I go and explore"), and modelled a mentalizing stance, in which the facilitator was playing with taking the baby's perspective. The facilitator also indirectly addressed the mother's possible tendency to put the baby into a parentifying role ("will *you* be alright"?). It also normalized the mother's hesitation in encountering a new group of other people ("we see that with all first-timers") and sought to respond to possible feelings of isolation and exclusion ("can you tell me about you and baby"), working to build a sense of trust and connectedness in the group. Linking the two mothers was an opportunity to attend to the real social isolation that many parents with young babies feel.

Use of play

Play is highly valued in a PPIP group as a way of helping parents and babies to bond in enjoyable and spontaneous ways. Sometimes a parent reports not knowing how to play, or comments that they were never played with themselves. In the group, play is also a central medium for creating the "interactive rhythm" of the group (James & Rosan, 2019). Parents and baby play, pause, watch others, join with others. Mobile babies play fleetingly with or alongside other baby and adult partners. The facilitators, scanning the room, can ascertain situations where play does not take place, or is repetitive, forced, no longer playful. Being in a group provides an opportunity for relaxed play to be modelled or supported by connecting up with others' play. Play and playfulness also link with celebrating the positive experiences of mastery or growth in the baby and/or parent. In this way accomplishments are witnessed and validated and pleasure and hope become embedded in the group as a whole, alongside difficulties.

Reflective practice

As a parallel to the process of post-session reflectivity discussed in Chapter 6, reflective discourse between the group facilitators is integral to, and critical to, the community group model – it is the forum for sharing concerns about risk and for restoring the facilitators' mentalizing processes. Often this is the most neglected aspect of delivery for many reasons: there are very real pressures on staff time, emergencies need to be dealt with, etc. There are often also psychological barriers to responding more directly to the pain or conflicts that emerge in the mother-infant group, or the stresses within the staff team facilitating the group. An atmosphere of trust needs to be consciously built up for a genuine exchange of observations, emotional responses and reflections.

Feedback from a children centre family worker described this process:

> I found the early months quite a strain. We are a small team but getting together after the group was really difficult. Everyone seemed to find something else they urgently needed to do. When we did sit together for discussion, nothing interesting happened so we joked around and left. Then A, the programme supervisor, joined us for a while and this set the tone. We found that on the whole we all worried about the same families and could plan for them together. Also, the input from another staff member, B, was really good – she saw things differently from me but I could learn from her.

Reflective discussion with peers that feels safe to the participants can also open a space to reflect on their own, not necessarily conscious or acknowledged, responses to situations. How did they feel? What did they "do" with these feelings? Have they found themselves becoming didactic with certain dyads or in certain situations? Or have they perhaps found themselves losing empathy, judging, becoming intrusive or alternatively avoiding? Gradually building an emotionally supportive and holding environment for the staff reinforces their ability to provide this for the families in the group and is reported to transfer into other areas of their practice. The open and curious thinking not only scaffolds the mentalizing approach brought to the group but the staff become more informally collaborative during the group sessions.

Setting up a group

The broad aims of a community group are to increase parental mentalizing of their babies, to increase positive parent-infant interactions and to train local, community-based staff to be baby-led in their interventions.

Structured, time-limited groups versus drop-in groups

Structured groups are normally closed, time-limited and directed towards a targeted population, for example, structured groups were developed for mother-baby units in prisons (Sleed, Baradon, & Fonagy, 2013). We will give an example of a closed group in the final section of this chapter.

In contrast, drop-in groups offer looser boundaries inasmuch as parents, although encouraged to attend regularly, are welcomed whether they are frequent or irregular attenders. This enables the parents to regulate their "dosage" according to their capacities and defences. It may, for example, be while waiting to be seen by the health visitor, or when joining a local place of worship or children's centre baby group.

Planning for delivery

Key to successful delivery is collaboration and partnership planning with commissioners, service users, those tasked to deliver the groups, and their supervisors. Buy-in is important at all levels, since whether a group flourishes or not depends on meeting the commissioning agenda, practitioner commitment, accessibility and service user engagement. We have found that it is not sufficient for one or two of the involved parties to embrace the programme, and that step-by-step building of ongoing working relationships can not only bring everyone around the table but also enrich the model by adapting it to local circumstances.

Evaluation

Evaluations need to be designed and budgeted for in the planning stage. It is best when the evaluation tools reflect the aims of the programme and when the tools are standardized outcome measures which enable comparison across populations and other studies. Evaluations can also be enhanced by conducting and analysing qualitative interviews with clients and staff. These populations may be particularly helpful in considering whether the programme has delivered what it hoped to deliver and whether the recipients think it was of value. Interviews with staff and managers will give information about the extent to which there has been a cultural change within the service to "think baby" and the development of increased skills in observing and intervening with babies.

Implementation as an iterative process

Regular reviews to monitor delivery and address problems collaboratively can sustain fidelity to the model and ensure outcomes in relation to aims. A review meeting may also support the refining of the programme to align it more closely with commissioner and client cultures. Moreover, when the model is delivered across a number of agencies in a locality, a peer-support culture can emerge from the review meeting, which positively influences delivery. For example, an unexpected problem of overcrowding arose in a baby clinic where mothers and babies started to stay in the clinic for longer in order to join the baby group. Discussion of this in the review meeting stimulated interest in arrangements in other baby clinics and also led to a practical solution for the overcrowded clinic.

Embedding PPIP-informed groups in the local services

In recent years there has been a shift away from commissioning outside "expert practitioners" to delivering a service that upskills the local workforce to deliver the programme. At the level of public policy, the benefits of such "train the trainer" endeavours are that local providers take ownership of the programme and infant mental health is promoted as a locally endorsed priority.

The move towards skill transfer from specialist to generic settings has implications for selection of facilitators, training and supervision, and fidelity to the model within the specific service environment and local culture.

Selection and training of group facilitators

A key criterion for selection is the interest and capacity of the individual practitioner to develop a new way of working. Often the best approach is to introduce the thinking and key ideas to potential group practitioners, to gauge their response and interest. Only with sufficient engagement and enthusiasm can a new approach get proper traction.

When it comes to training, the selected practitioners are introduced to key concepts of infant development, the parent-infant relationship and group ideas and dynamics. In their practice they are trained to observe and reflect, to represent the baby, and focus on the parent-infant relationship. Reflective practice is incorporated into the experience-based training, a way of working which may differ from the approach to which the practitioners are accustomed from facilitating psycho-educational groups with individual mothers or mother-infant dyads.

Supervision

Supervision offers both personal and team development in this paradigm. Supervisors who combine PPIP and group expertise are still a scarce resource but are ideal candidates. PPIP expertise is essential for expanding facilitator understanding of unconscious processes in the parent-infant relationship, and proficiency in running groups extends the possibilities of building on the group as an attachment figure for the participants. Once again, a "train the trainer" approach can be applied to build up local peer support. However, peer support often operates at a different level to supervision and there can be slippage in terms of adherence to the original model. One of our informal findings from supervising group facilitators is that they tend not to challenge each other's practice too closely. This is understandable in terms of ongoing work relationships but does mean that more difficult conversations tend to be avoided.

Fidelity of implementation

Adherence to the model is important in terms of achievement of the desired outcomes. However, research also shows that fidelity often decreases over time (Elliott & Mihalic, 2004). Informal feedback has taught us that the key message and idea that practitioners retain is the centrality of the baby – the baby-led approach tends to be understood and embraced. A second idea that is often held onto is the importance of careful observation of the interactive back and forth between parent and infant. And third, practitioners report they have learnt the importance of trying to combat the inclination to be critical of the parents, while holding on to the ability to recognize risk. As mentioned, one of the elements that often seems to get lost is that of maintaining reflective discourse after the group. Lack of time is usually the explanation, although we also have feedback about the challenges of maintaining the emotional safety of a peer discussion group.

There is also the dilemma of maintaining the model's fidelity versus adapting to the local environment in which the intervention is being implemented. Areas and agencies differ in the fiscal and human resources available to respond to differing levels of local need, cultural norms within different resident and user groupings, availability of qualified staff, etc. It is most useful to address these issues when planning implementation so that appropriate flexibility can be built into the aims and method of delivery, while holding on to the essential framework.

An example of a community-based programme: New Beginnings

We finish this chapter with a description of a community-based intervention for high-risk infants and mothers, New Beginnings (NB). As a PPIP intervention, NB is informed by psychoanalytic ideas and expanded by attachment and mentalization perspectives (Baradon et al., 2017). In the following discussion, for the purposes of the dialogue of this book, we emphasize the mentalization concepts.

NB was initially developed for mothers and babies in Mother-Baby Units (MBUs) in prisons. Incarcerated mothers are a high-risk group in relation to both past and current trauma (Borelli, Goshin, Joestl, Clark, & Byrne, 2010) (Zlotnick, Najavits, Rohsenow, & Johnson, 2003), and NB was developed to support this highly vulnerable population of mother-infant dyads (Baradon, Fonagy, Bland, Lénárd, & Sleed, 2008; Sleed, Baradon, et al., 2013). Because of the high turnover in MBUs, NB was originally developed as a relatively short and focused programme, involving an 8-week intervention consisting of intensive weekly sessions for 6 weeks, with the first and last meetings being used to administer outcomes measures (Baradon & Target, 2010). Following a pilot trial, NB was put into practice in a cluster randomized trial in four major MBUs (Sleed, Baradon, et al., 2013).

In 2012, NB was adapted for practice in community settings by locally employed staff, so that resources are built up within community statutory services. It is the Community NB (NB-C) that we describe here to provide a real-life example of the kind of group practice we have discussed in principle so far in this chapter.

NB-C was developed as an intervention for families who are at a point where authorities are actively concerned about the functioning of the family and the separation of the child from their family is being considered. Some of these families have previously had children removed from their care and this is a moment of considerable pressure for the parent/parents, which in some cases may add to motivation to participate but can also add to difficulties around heightened stress and low levels of trust towards helping systems. Protection concerns and responsibilities also mean that the professionals and care networks involved are at heightened alert at this stage.

Partly in response to the high levels of vigilance and issues at stake while working with this group, NB-C was developed as a structured and manualized time-limited group intervention. Its overall aim is to enhance parental mentalizing in relation to self, baby and the relationship between them. NB-C is delivered by two facilitators and each group has up to six mother-infant dyads. Facilitators are social workers and clinical psychologists employed by the Social Care services who have a background in working with families and infants, but have not necessarily undegone specialist training in infant mental health.

NB-C treatment provides 16 sessions, across about 4 months. The first two sessions are made up of individual meetings between group facilitators and potential group members to engage the parents' interest in the programme, to create a personal relationship and to administer initial evaluation measures.

The following twelve sessions are group sessions run on consecutive weeks. Each session is structured around a topic. The topics were selected on the basis of evidence for their potential to activate the attachment relationship. The subjects cover the history of the pregnancy, the family tree of the baby, mother's representations of her own childhood experiences, her aspirations for herself and her baby, and separations. The sequence of session topics has been planned sensitively, beginning with topics that are often easier for mothers to tolerate and reflect upon – for example, "how does my baby learn about his world?" – progressing to more emotionally painful topics, such as relationships with fathers. Each session is 90 minutes long, but is part of a wider morning's programme of activities, which involves an informal play session before the group (with facilitators and any partners who wish to join), and lunch afterwards. These activities support the work of the programme and provide a regulating scaffold around the more emotionally intensive work of the group session. Participants are asked to attend sessions regularly with their babies, and to stay in the session.

Two individual feedback sessions are held to discuss progress and issues to be addressed – the first mid and the second at the end.

The aims of NB-C are:

1. To extend mothers' capacity to think about their babies' intersubjective and attachment needs as separate from their own.
2. To mobilize genuine emotional interest between mother and baby.
3. To broaden the adults' contingent responsivity to their babies' communications.
4. To enhance the baby's attachment behaviours towards their mothers.

The adult-oriented, mentalization-informed clinical tools used by NB are: observation of individual, dyadic and group behaviours, communications, transactions and states of mind; group discussion between all the adults of attachment-related topics presented in the formal content of the programme and linked reflective discussions about the observations; and psycho-educational handouts. Infant-oriented interventions include marked mirroring, labelling affect and making links, and age-appropriate play.

Many of the mothers have experienced criticism, social isolation and bullying, and come to the group apprehensively. The facilitators urge the participants to co-construct a group in which listening, acknowledging and respecting each other confound transference expectations of rejection. As the group coheres, the mothers increasingly recruit each other into more authentic sharing and reflective exchanges, and some can begin to sensitively challenge the rigid representations held by others in a way that may be too threatening if done by a facilitator. This mother-to-mother interaction, while sometimes uncomfortable, can significantly strengthen the individual's sense of worth in relation to others in the group.

The group element is also of crucial importance for the babies. A "baby group" is spontaneously created in its own right as the infants explore and respond to one another and form connections. Their curiosity and antics can bring a lively perspective on development. The facilitators help mothers to view the babies as separate social beings, and this is further reinforced by ongoing observations of the other infants. Discussions about the babies' group processes can foster greater awareness in the mothers of the babies' responses to their actions, evoking surprise, pride and pleasure. Mothers can visibly take on aspects of attuned and sensitive care demonstrated by other members of the group and/or modelled by facilitators.

Many of the women in NB-C will have been inadequately mentalized as infants and children in precisely a way that generates the epistemic freezing that can make them so hard to help through conventional services. The accumulating effects of social adversity and alienation from the institutions they encounter and the culture they inhabit will have made such epistemic closure a highly understandable adaptation. The work of NB-C is to create an environment in which epistemic trust can be re-opened in the parents

Through the content of the programme, as elaborated and interactively personalized in the sessions, NB-C implicitly provides the parents with a meaningful model of mind and an understanding of their own and their babies' singular development, as well as an idea of the process of change. At a group level there is a transactional and gradual development of a culture whereby the parents entrust the practitioner, and each other, with aspects of their vulnerability and helplessness, and the facilitator reliably helps to hold painful emotions and create meaning out of experience (Sleed, Baradon, et al., 2013). For this critical sense of "genuineness" to pervade the group, the facilitators need to model their own authentic mentalizing processes – observing, listening, and reflecting – and their capacity to be open to their own thoughts and responses, consistently enquiring in a non-judgemental way the difficulties and uncertainties that are intrinsic to mentalization. In their facial expressions, tone of voice and body cues as much as in what each person says, the facilitators will be communicating their attitudes.

Moreover, the facilitators are careful to be explicit in their mentalizing stance (see Chapter 5) – talking in a direct, emotionally genuine way, providing explanations for what they are doing at each step of the programme, making their thinking available to the participants ("I am saying this because I noticed a few times that . . ."). The facilitators acknowledge the women's experience of them and also their behaviours that may have contributed to hitches, and consider with the group how they may work together towards re-establishing trust when it has been disrupted. For many of the women, a readiness on the part of the facilitators to recognize their own contributions to an interaction will come as a surprise. The process of "interactive repair" (Tronick & Weinberg, 1997), whereby mismatches or misunderstanding are recognized, acknowledged and addressed, mirrors the kind of work mothers and babies need to do together to repair mismatches between them. Experiencing this in a group can help normalize both errors and repair.

An intervention in the NB-C group may draw on an observation of an ordinary, brief, in-the-moment sequence between mother and baby to engage the whole group in thinking about the meaning of what has just happened for the dyad and each partner in it, and to be meaningful to others in the group. For example, the facilitator puts her observation to the mother and the group: "Joseph (baby) fretted, you offered him the breast, he looked at you, into your face, but did not latch on" (an example of mismatch). The facilitator then opens the observation for reflection: "I wonder what stopped Joseph from latching on?" (an open mentalizing question). The group offers different thoughts – some thinking sympathetically about mother, some curious about baby, and others holding to concrete ideas about feeding.

The facilitator addresses Joseph, speaking slowly and nodding her head, summarizing and slightly extending the group's suggestions:

> We think that Mummy wants to feed you when you are hungry so that your tummy doesn't hurt and you grow big and strong . . . [Validating mother's positive intentions, acknowledging mid-range contingency in that mother is seen to recognize her baby's cues, rather than intrude or ignore]. But perhaps you felt mummy's tension when

she offered you her breast, because her nipple is very cracked . . . And maybe you need to see mummy's face reassure you that it is OK to hurt her if you are hungry and you will both be OK. [Emphasizing authentic communication between the dyad, disruption and repair].

Setting-up NB-C

Partnership planning

The mentalizing approach was extended to the planning and monitoring of the programme with the relevant bodies. The starting point was a process of consultation: focus groups and individual meetings were held with the programme facilitators, commissioners, and service users to review the programme, learn from experience and plan for sensitive, local delivery.

Each of these groups made important contributions. For example, mothers who had participated in the programme recommended adaptations to make certain elements more user-friendly. These were endorsed by the facilitators, who also fed back those aspects of the programme that worked well, in their view, and those aspects which were not sufficiently sensitive to the mothers' states of mind or group dynamics. The commissioners were invested in the use of NB as an intervention which could inform their decision-making process regarding their most worrying families. To accommodate their agenda, we built in formal but transparent procedures for feedback to professionals while boundaries for preserving appropriate confidentiality of the participants were built into the programme. The focus groups with potential service users, which were held with local mothers of babies, placed particular emphasis on engagement and supporting participants to complete the programme. They brought to the discussion both realistic difficulties (such as transport and finances) and personal narratives of discouragement and disengagement due to shame, a feeling of being judged, and of being targeted, and had ideas about how these may be addressed in implementing the programme. On the basis of discussions with them, there was an emphasis on increased flexibility in building the relationships with each mother and baby (e.g., telephone calls and messages, home visits when necessary) to accommodate their histories of disrupted attachments and difficulties in sustaining ongoing investment in a group in which attachments are the focus of attention.

Evaluation

The aims of the evaluation were also agreed in partnership with the commissioners as well programme planners at the AFC. The AFC's objectives were to evaluate the effectiveness of the intervention against the programme's aims. To this the commissioners added objectives related to enhancing decision-making with regards to the final care plan for the baby and improving the skill set of the facilitators.

Embedding the programme in the local services

Whereas NB had previously been delivered in prison Mother-Baby Units by the Anna Freud Centre as an external body, with the complexities and advantages this brought (Tomas-Merrills & Chakraborty, 2010), the aim was to embed the community programme within local services. This was considered advantageous for a number of reasons. At the level of planning and implementation, the local statutory services were involved in decisions about key areas: staffing, facilities and budget, evaluation design, defining the inclusion criteria, recruitment and engagement processes, feedback model and management of risk. On the level of public policy, it was felt that with the statutory providers taking ownership of the programme, infant mental health would become a locally endorsed priority.

Creating a "think baby" organizational culture

A central tenet of all mentalization-based approaches is that reflectiveness within the broad professional network is critical to making an impact at the individual level; in other words, mentalizing cannot occur in isolation (Bevington, Fuggle, Fonagy, Target, & Asen, 2013; Midgley & Vrouva, 2013). This was deemed to be of particular importance in the context of the Social Services system, where child protection requirements predominate. For this reason, an initial phase of training was provided to a broad cross-section of the staff group working with these families. The objective was to raise awareness of relational development and difficulties in infancy and to promote a more knowledgeable and thoughtful approach to working with parents and infants. Thus, the main principles were embedded into the organizational culture, an important element of the model, since all families in the NB-C groups are referred and supported by the broader staff alongside the programme.

Training of facilitators

The training of the service staff contributed to skill transfer from specialist to generic settings – from the Anna Freud Centre to local services. Within the broader upskilling of the professional workforce employed by the local authority, training and supervising of selected social workers and psychologists as NB facilitators created a more specialized core who, in time, took over infant mental health trainings within the service.

Facilitators are clinically trained professional (psychologists, social workers) chosen on the basis of interest and experience in parent – infant work and with groups, ability to assimilate a clinical-therapeutic focus in their work and ability to work collaboratively in co-facilitating the programme. The personal stance of the facilitator in imbuing a sense of interest, safety and sensitivity is critical. Facilitators who offer a sense of authenticity and commitment construct a stronger foundation for change to occur.

Facilitators are expected to model an open, trusting relationship between collaborating adults to the mothers and babies, where domestic friction is a common occurrence. Therefore, their working relationship is central to the programme and is attended to in the selection process and in supervision.

Implementation as an iterative process

The local service management is usually highly invested in maximizing the contributions of the programme to the execution of their legal responsibilities. Therefore, regular reviews are held with them to monitor delivery in relation to local client and organizational culture. These meetings were helpful to the Anna Freud Centre in refining the programme, and to the local authority in terms of reliability of input to their care processes. Similar processes take place with professional and client focus groups.

Clinical supervision

Weekly supervision is provided to the facilitators during the course of the programme as a reflective space, to maintain safety, therapeutic efficacy and adherence to the NB-C programme. Central in this is the need to process highly arousing experiences generated by the individual histories of the mothers and babies and the group dynamics. Supervision also helps to monitor unconscious attempts by the parents to recruit the facilitators into a worldview that may be indicative of split-off and defensive processes and to maintain awareness of how these are acted upon, sometimes in the facilitator relationship. Supervision is a forum to formulate ways to manage such processes in the group, and to consider how this might influence systemic and risk factors. Tension between facilitators – whether interpersonal or due to group processes or, for example, one of them being less experienced in working with dyads – is also addressed within supervision.

References

Baradon, T., Fonagy, P., Bland, K., Lénárd, K., & Sleed, M. (2008). New Beginnings: An experience-based programme addressing the attachment relationship between mothers and their babies in prisons. *Journal of Child Psychotherapy, 34*(2), 240–258. Doi:10.1080/00754170802208065

Baradon, T., Sleed, M., Atkins, R., Campbell, C., Fagin, A., Van Schaick, R., & Fonagy, P. (2017). New beginnings: A time-limited, group intervention for high-risk infants and mothers. In H. Steele & M. Steele (Eds.), *Handbook of attachment-based interventions*. New York, NY: Guilford Press.

Baradon, T., & Target, T. (2010). New beginnings: A psychoanalytically informed programme to support primary attachment relationships between mothers and babies in prison. In A. Lemma & M. Patrick (Eds.), *Off the couch: Contemporary psychoanalytic applications* (pp. 11–81). London: Routledge.

Bateman, A., Campbell, C., Luyten, P., & Fonagy, P. (2018). A mentalization-based approach to common factors in the treatment of borderline personality disorder. *Current Opinion in Psychology, 21*, 44–49. Doi:10.1016/j.copsyc.2017.09.005

Bevington, D., Fuggle, P., Fonagy, P., Target, M., & Asen, E. (2013). Innovations in practice: Adolescent Mentalization-Based Integrative Therapy (AMBIT): A new integrated approach to working with the most hard to reach adolescents with severe complex mental health needs. *Child and Adolescent Mental Health, 18*(1), 46–51. Doi:10.1111/j.1475-3588.2012.00666.x

Borelli, J. L., Goshin, L. S., Joestl, S., Clark, J., & Byrne, M. W. (2010). Attachment organization in a sample of incarcerated mothers: Distribution of classifications and associations with substance abuse history, depressive symptoms, perceptions of parenting competency and social support. *Attachment and Human Development, 12*(4), 355–374.

Elliott, D. S., & Mihalic, S. (2004). Issues in disseminating and replicating effective prevention programs. *Prevention Science, 5*(1), 47–53. Doi:10.1023/b:prev.0000013981.28071.52

Fonagy, P., Campbell, C., Constantinou, M., Higgitt, A., Allison, E., & Luyten, P. (2021). Culture and psychopathology. *Development and Psychopathology*, 1–16. Doi:10.1017/S0954579421000092

Hogg, S., Haines, A., Baradon, T., & Cuthbert, C. (2015). *An unstable start: All babies count: Spotlight on homelessness*. NSPCC's All Babies Count campaign, UK.

James, J. (2016). Parent-infant psychotherapy in groups. In T. Baradon, M. Biseo, C. Broughton, J. James, & A. Joyce (Eds.), *The practice of psychoanalytic parent-infant psychotherapy: Claiming the baby* (2nd ed., pp. 138–157). London: Routledge.

James, J., & Rosan, C. (2019). Remodelling baby clinics: Opportunities to support parent–baby relationships. *Journal of Health Visiting, 7*(8), 400–404. Doi:10.12968/johv.2019.7.8.400

Midgley, N., & Vrouva, I. (Eds.). (2013). *Minding the child: Mentalization-based interventions with children, young people and their families*. London, UK: Routledge.

Sleed, M., Baradon, T., & Fonagy, P. (2013). New beginnings for mothers and babies in prison: A cluster randomized controlled trial. *Attachment and Human Development, 15*(4), 349–367. Doi:10.1080/14616734.2013.782651

Sleed, M., James, J., Baradon, T., Newbery, J., & Fonagy, P. (2013). A psychotherapeutic baby clinic in a hostel for homeless families: Practice and evaluation. *Psychol Psychother, 86*(1), 1–18. Doi:10.1111/j.2044-8341.2011.02050.x

Tomas-Merrills, J., & Chakraborty, A. (2010). Babies behind bars: Working with relational trauma with mothers and babies in prison. In T. Baradon (Ed.), *Relational trauma in infancy: Psychoanalytic, attachment and neuropsychological contributions to parent-infant psychotherapy* (pp. 103–115). Hove, UK: Routledge.

Tronick, E., & Weinberg, M. K. (1997). Depressed mothers and infants: Failure to form dyadic consciousness. In L. Murray & P. Cooper (Eds.), *Postpartum depression and child development*. New York: Guilford Press.

Zlotnick, C., Najavits, L. M., Rohsenow, D. J., & Johnson, D. M. (2003). A cognitive-behavioral treatment for incarcerated women with substance abuse disorder and posttraumatic stress disorder: Findings from a pilot study. *Journal of Substance Abuse Treatment, 25*(2), 99–105.

9 Practitioner challenges and rewards

We have made clear our view that working with infants and their families where there is serious disturbance requires expert knowledge and practice and ongoing supervisory support. In this section we consider both the potential rewards and aspects of the work that present particular challenges to those working in the field of infant mental health. It is these challenges that underpin the argument for a perinatal specialism within all infant mental health practice, including psychotherapy.

Working with infancy

It can be a profound experience to work with a very young infant and a new parent to support their coupling, and to help a triad to come together as a family. Undoubtably, it has reparative resonance for everyone – we all once sought safety in a parent and loved them for it. Moreover, despite the intensity of early anxieties, the potential for relatively rapid but significant change characterizes the perinatal period. As Daws has pointed out, a little bit of help can sometimes go a long way (Mind to Mind interview). For example:

> A mother with painful inflammation of her nipples was trying to breast feed her 3- day old infant. "Open your mouth" she said to him, "Yawwn", "get on with it". The baby fussed and did not feed. The therapist saw the baby was looking at mother's face which was half hidden by the full breast that was looming over him. "He is more interested in your face" she said in a warm, engaging voice. "Ah" said Mother and she shifted Baby so he could look fully at her. The urgency of "getting it done and over with" lessened tangibly as she smiled and cooed to him. After a few seconds mother said gently "are you ready now?" and Baby took the nipple with gusto.

DOI: 10.4324/9781003024323-9

This intervention demonstrates how an understanding of unconscious processes and of infant attachment needs can be translated into an affirmation of ordinary relating. What stands out is the simplicity of the intervention yet its depth in capturing the baby's need to know that he can, indeed, "attack" the breast with his appetite and mother will survive, and the mother's wish for an emotional bond with her baby beyond the feed. The intervention helped moved both mother and baby from states of persecutory anxiety to mutuality. In terms of mentalizing practice, we see the emphasis on affective/cognitive aspects of the baby's experience in the here-and-now, rather than an interpretative casting of the possible reasons for not latching on (e.g., the mother's mixed communication: do feed, but it will damage me).

Supportive and therapeutic work is aided by the developmental thrust of the baby and the psychological reorganization of the perinatal period in the parent/parents. Babies seem able to utilize therapeutic input to keep their attachment pathways open: they quickly realize the interest and concern of the therapist and turn to the therapist when support is not forthcoming from the parent. For their part, parents who engage with an intervention carry a genuine wish to do well by their infants and when a previously withdrawn, conflicted or otherwise unavailable parent becomes more responsive, the baby quickly loses interest in the therapist and directs their love and gratitude to the parent.

With regards to PPIP, because this therapeutic modality explores both parents' and babies' inner worlds and experiences, concomitant processes of discovery and development are intimately shared with and by the therapist. The therapist is on the floor with baby and parents, amidst the fluids, odours, excretions, mess, appetite and emotional vehemence of infancy and caretaking. S/he partakes in the melee of the here-and-now without the conventional furniture of adult and child analysis – the couch or chair, free association and symbolic play. It can be deeply moving and interesting to work at this proximity and, at the same, this level of exposure can feel intense and personal. This approach could be encouraged in mentalization-based parent-infant work where, traditionally, the pull may be to work with the parent's representations and mentalizing capacities. In the chapters of this book, we have emphasized the importance of directly mentalizing the baby to support his or her developmental thrust.

Raw emotions, early states of mind

Earliest states of mind are urgent, intense and potentially unbearable, such that the individual may desperately struggle to contain or alleviate them. Raphael-Leff quotes a new mother on her analytic couch: "I'm climbing the walls . . . I don't know how to survive this" (Raphael-Leff, 2000). Raphael-Leff continues "we see a mother tending her baby but internally she is being engulfed by what is 'closing in' inside – unprocessed, acute moments with her own, fallible, early caregivers, now revitalised in the demanding arena of babycare" (Raphael-Leff, 2000, p. 60). We have described our conceptualization of babies' internal sensations of dependency, vulnerability and "disintegrating" and "falling forever" when under psychic threat. Working with such concrete feelings, pitched at such high stakes, can impact the therapist at many levels. At the level of our own attachment responses, seeing parents and babies in extreme emotional pain and tension with each other is very difficult. Such urgent intensity of feelings can also be contagious and may resonate with earliest states in the therapist – hitherto analysed or defended against. Furthermore, these states of mind are related to fight, flight, freeze, collapse and hyper-vigilant states; these bodily expressive and enactive situations can undermine the therapist's ability to use their own independent thinking. In situations of high arousal, particularly of negative affect and conflict, mentalizing capacities are reduced making it harder to regain emotional balance. Our microanalytic research has shown how difficult (but of course crucial) this is when a distressed baby is involved. Guilt and/or an attachment driven wish to console the other (as well as self) can really complicate internal processing of the arousal.

The challenge for practitioners is to remain open to being affected by, and responsive to, these feeling states in the self as well as the other (rather than defending against them) and to hold on to a measure of reflectivity when emotionally aroused themselves.

Holding infant and parent/parents in mind

As mentioned in Chapter 1, the ability to hold both the infant and his or her parent/parents and their relationship in mind is considered the core infant mental health competency. It requires what we have loosely called a split vision, and regular self-monitoring by the therapist of his or her attentional drift and intensified identifications. Naturally, there will be times when the therapist catches him/herself having focused almost exclusively on one with the other lost from mind. The information lost will be primarily of the state of mind of the other. For example, how does the infant respond to his mother's crying, is it different to his reactions when she speaks about her partner in an angry tone? There is also the danger that the infant will experience the therapist's intense focus on his mother as a loss of selfhood, repeating the experiences he has when his mother becomes consumed by her own concerns. How to attend to two (or three) patients is a frequent question at the beginning of training, but this ability grows through training and the maturity of a PPIP therapist, and through self-monitoring.

Embodied communication

Working with parents and infants requires the practitioner to be alert to embodied communication, including their own, when, in fact, so much of our body expressivity is procedural and out of consciousness. We are much more able to recall what we said than how we said it or what our bodies were doing and how we may have come across to our partners in dialogue. Even in trainings, teaching/learning about the therapist's embodied communications mostly does not feature and we are simply not adept at embodied self-knowledge when we qualify. Moreover, analytic therapists often develop internal parameters regarding professional non-verbal communication and may feel uncomfortable when that frame becomes more fluid, as it does in PPIP. For these reasons, a significant element of the process of learning the PPIP model comes from watching videoed sessions of ourselves at work. There seems to be a natural learning trajectory for the trainees. At first the focus is on observing gesture, sequence, rhythm and such detailed constituents of the interactions between parent/parents and infant in order to make sense of the relationship. With accruing experience, the attention can shift to watching oneself "in-action". We quote here feedback from a trainee in the PPIP programme:

> I have been a PPIP trainee for 16 months and over this period I have taken video sessions to supervision. As a trained psychotherapist, I had a sense of myself in the room with children and couples (as) someone calm and reasonably containing. I also thought, and still think, that one of my strengths is my ability to use countertransference as a way of understanding what was happening in the room. So, it was a surprise for me when I watched the video session with my supervisor and peer group to see how loudly my body spoke its mind, unconsciously of course. I became aware of how my body expressed my defences, such as how I might sit or change positions, pull my legs to my body as if protecting myself or closing my body to the parent and infant. I came to understand how my defensive use of my body may be keeping at bay the distressing feeling states of the babies (who) expressed themselves through their bodies, through skin irritations, ear infections, colds etc. They communicated through their bodies what they were unable to put into words. (Sara Leon, Infant, Child, Adolescent, Couple Therapist)

As this trainee so acutely notes, observing one's own bodily communication can feel like catching sight of the unconscious. It may feel exposing, upsetting but also illuminating. In many trainees, it stimulates self-reflection and change. To again quote a trainee:

> Sharing the footage in supervision can feel raw, embarrassing, exposing and frightening. The rewards of the others' in-depth perspectives always outweigh the initial costs, however, and sharing a moment of change or delightful interaction, which would otherwise never be witnessed by another, is a genuine joy within this model of working.

The heightened awareness of embodied communication extends also to the embodied transference and countertransference, as the following vignette illustrates:

> Ayad (eight months) made his way towards the therapist. Mother smiled and nodded to the rhythm of her infant's crawl. He stopped at about an arm's length from the therapist and gazed at him, then smiled. The therapist smiled back in an open way, and Ayad reached out to touch his hand. But then Ayad dropped his hand, looking intensely at the therapist, and slowly backed away.

Watching the video after the session, the therapist noticed that he (therapist) had withdrawn slightly when Ayad got right up to him; in an unconscious movement in the moment, the therapist had given the baby a message: "to here, but no further". He was surprised to see that prohibiting gesture of his but remembered feeling concerned that mother would have disapproved had he allowed her baby to explore him further. The therapist watched the video a second time, with his supervisor. This time he noticed something else: as the baby got right up to him, mother had tapped the baby's bottom lightly. This message "no further" had initially been hidden behind her smile. He was amazed to see that mother's gesture and his withdrawal were coordinated in time. It is important that these embodied communications, through which the therapist was alerted to mother's non-triangulated transference to him, occurred too rapidly to be registered consciously, but influenced the trajectory between all three of them. In terms of mentalization-based parent–infant therapy, this vignette highlights the importance of embodied mentalization in earliest relationships, and the need for infant therapists to familiarize themselves with nonverbal mentalizing frameworks such as Parental Embodied Mentalizing Assessment. Working with such forms and expressions of mentalizing is something of a change in focus from the emphasis on thoughts and cognitions in MBT practice but are essential in engaging with an infant's subjectivity.

Transference to the therapist

Two relatively common situations in parent-infant psychotherapy are the emergence of a negative transference and idealization in relation to the therapist. How and when to address a parent's negative transference to the therapist is a thorny issue in parent-infant psychotherapy because of potential risk to the baby, either by the parent's withdrawal from the therapy and/or the risk the parent will transfer their hostility from the therapist to the baby (or partner). A cautious approach advocates addressing the negative transference if it threatens the therapy or impinges on the parent-infant relationship. A different approach uses the ongoing frame of therapy, such as breaks, to address transference feelings of disappointment, disillusion, anger, etc. Sometimes the negative transference is taken up directly, but other times it may be taken up via the parent-infant relationship, as the following example shows:

> The session started with three-month-old Saoirse screaming and mother and therapist observably tense, as the move from waiting to consulting rooms had entailed an interruption of a feed. Mother immediately offered the breast muttering a rather impatient "I know, I know" and Saoirse latched on hard, as though an ordinary (plentiful) flow of milk would not suffice, so she was pulling the milk into her. The therapist kicked off her shoes crying out "sorry, sorry" as she joined them on the mat. Her apology was non-specific, thus both mother and baby could feel it was personalised to themselves, or not. Her tone of voice as she apologised was high pitched and urgent, it matched the baby's state of upset and anger about the disruption of her feed (in which mother felt to her as the depriving object) and mother's feelings in the face of her baby's state.

For the mother, the narrative seemed to coalesce around blame: the therapist was to blame for the baby's distress. It was a familiar narrative wherein mother's ambivalence towards her own mother played out in her finger pointing at the "damaging" therapist. But the therapist elected to not to address the conflictual transference and rather to help with the mother's implicit guilt towards her very young baby for failing as a mother – "sorry" perhaps representing the other side of the "I know" coin.

Idealization of the therapist is another complex aspect of transferences in PPIP. While idealization may certainly be defensive (e.g., warding off the anticipated attack of the "bad" object) sometimes it may need to be accepted. It can be seen as part and parcel of the clinical process of shielding the child as well as the therapeutic work while a benign mother is being internalized. Sometimes, the idealization represents a parent's dependence on the therapist as an auxiliary ego while s/he struggles with their own as well as their infant's emotional rawness and volatility. For example, a mother told her therapist that she was proud to have managed her panic to the point that she had been able to console her baby when he cried. She exclaimed: "you are the mother I never had", that is, one who helped her put into place building blocks for emotional regulation. It is important to be open to the patient/s' – parent's and infant's – need to experience the analyst's capacity to receive their love. This is particularly significant when a parent is unable to accept their baby's love, for example when masochism or hostility may blind them to their infant's passion.

While it is important to recognize that the gratitude a patient feels in response to alleviation of their distress can contribute to idealization, it can also require the therapist to examine his or her countertransference and what has been implicitly conveyed to the parent and infant. Idealization may reflect the therapist's own need to be "special" to the family. These matters are complex, and some sorting out may have to be done. For example:

> A male therapist worked over a couple of years with a mother and her child born of rape. After a week's break, the toddler ran towards him in the waiting room calling excitedly "Daddy, Daddy". Her mother looked beseechingly at the therapist.

This was a troubling situation for the therapist. He understood that the child's action expressed her loving feelings towards him as the only reliable and warm father-figure she had. He was also aware of her mother's real thankfulness for his reliable presence as well as her loneliness and hunger for a protective partner. The dilemma was how to accept their "love" and yet re-establish the boundaries of reality around the phantasy. The therapist also wondered whether he may have colluded with this in his deeply felt compassion for this dyad and had perhaps been "nudged" (Sandler, 1976) into contributing to their shared wishful phantasy that he would complete their isolated, one parent family unit.

The therapist as a new object

Whether the therapist can offer him or herself as a new object (see Chapter 3) depends on the authenticity of her/his communications. Authenticity is the quality of being genuine or real, in the way the mother and father are required to be by their infant. This necessitates a measure of porousness to the other's "gaze" as much as reflection on oneself. An example of this can be seen in relation to the interactive repair of ruptures between therapist and parent or baby. Because so many of the parents who attend PPIP have been the subject of blame and humiliation in their childhoods and have scathing superegos which belittle their ongoing relationship endeavours, the therapist has to be careful not to collude with the internal self-critical voice of the parent. Holding in mind that all relationships are co-constructed, and that the mental state of the other can never be known with total certainty, therapists have to be open to the possibility that they, too, may have stumbled in their relating. This has emerged as a critical reparative factor in PPIP. When the therapist gives genuine consideration to his or her possible part in any miscommunication, s/he models a new way of relating in which open and genuine transactions are privileged, confounding intergenerational transference expectancies of blaming and shaming. This approach is fundamental in MBT as well, as captured in the idea of the mentalizing stance (Chapter 5).

The following illustration comes from an early PPIP session with a couple and their baby. The therapist had registered a withdrawal of the father at the very end of the previous session, expressed in an over-hasty exist. She followed this incident up during the next session.

THERAPIST: I have been thinking about what happened at the end of the last session. My impression was that something went wrong because (turning to the father) I saw you leaving abruptly and in haste. Was I right in in thinking that you were upset or disturbed by what I had said, or perhaps how I had said it?
  Baby babbles
TH (to baby and parents): yes, perhaps I was clumsy in how I spoke . . .
FATHER: I suddenly felt I was not welcome here
TH pauses to consider this, then asks: Can you tell me how that feeling came about?
FATHER (glancing at his partner): You looked very intense
TH NODS: I recognise that in myself
FATHER: My father could be very preachy. I always felt I was in the wrong. I really resent him for the insecurity I feel now
MOTHER: I am so relieved you talked about this rather than just dropping out as you usually do

In our view, what enabled the interactive repair between father and therapist was the therapist's genuine wish to understand her own contribution – inadvertent but nonetheless existent against the background of the father's transferential propensity to feel criticized. In mentalizing terms, we can again see a form of the mentalizing stance being expressed in the therapist's open questioning about the father's state of mind, while acknowledging that the therapist's position is tentative and cannot be certain ("am I right?", "perhaps"). The therapist's admission of their own role in the process ("I recognize that in myself") also modelled the mentalizing emphasis on the therapist openly accepting their roles in creating mismatches, or mentalizing failures. Indeed, a more explicitly mentalizing approach might have involved the therapist discussing the meaning of their "intense" expression and how it made the father feel in more detail, or would perhaps revisit this point later.

Another area of challenge potentially lies with the therapist's interventions with the baby. Many therapists in training are reluctant to engage too closely with the baby for fear of setting themselves up as rivals to the mother or as the "better parent" who thus evokes further sense of failure, and sometimes envy, in the parent. Rather than circumventing the issue by limiting the therapist's vitality in relation to the baby (making himself or herself less "attractive" to the baby), the therapist needs to be alert to the possibility that the parent may feel undermined and that, if this is indeed what happens, it can be spoken about with genuine interest and compassion. Such an approach can help the parent feel better equipped to partner collaboratively with other important figures in their child's life, such as their partner, peers and teachers.

Working with a triad

Working with baby and two parents in a room is complex. It is

> a psychological stretch for the therapist to attend to three bodies, minds, ghosts etc., which present a contemporaneous flow of narratives and needs. Indeed, even experienced therapists can feel overloaded by the totality of material and the dynamics of the family system in a session.
>
> (Baradon, 2019)

A partner's presence also brings couple dynamics to the therapy. Working with a couple's stresses can be a necessary component of PPIP since the perinatal period often introduces a dip in marital satisfaction, and yet the quality of the couple relationship impacts both their individual mental health and that of their baby (Salomonsson, 2018). However, some couples confront the therapist with levels of conflict that feel challenging when the baby is in the room, or even beyond his or her competence. The therapist's ability to conduct the therapeutic work may also be complicated when the couple bring different transferences or, indeed, split the positive and negative between them. One parent may bring a positive transference that steers a strong working alliance, while the other parent may hold a position of mistrust. The challenge to the therapist is to find a potential meeting point if the triadic work is to continue. Despite the complexities of working with a triad, its rewards lie in helping the three forge themselves into a family together.

Working with the triad also raises a question as to how comfortable the therapist is with the sexual overtones associated with the presence of the progenitors in the room: "The baby is a concrete representation of intercourse and introduces the couple's real sexuality and fecundity into the consulting room" (Baradon, 2019, p. 91). For example:

> Mother asked for home-visits as her back had been affected by the birth and she was immobile. The therapist was taken to couple's bedroom, where mother was convalescing. Initially, the therapist felt comfortable enough in that setting and felt that the PPIP work focused on integrating the baby into the family could take place. After a month or so, with the regularly unmade bed, stale smell, clothes on the floor, the therapist felt ill at ease in the bedroom, intruded upon in her professional mentalizing by the concreteness of the parents' sexuality. The therapist discussed this in supervision. She felt that the parents were presenting her with their sexuality as the glue to the relationship in the face of the invasion of the baby. Despite understanding this, it was felt that the therapy needed to move out of the bedroom to a consulting room. However, at this point the couple separated. Undoubtably the therapy was caught up in the couple dynamics.

Risk

The question of risk to the baby or his/her parents is always borne in mind and, because of the vulnerability of an infant, can weigh heavily on a therapist when there are concerns. A parent's fear that their baby will be removed is commonly brought into the consulting room, even if not verbalized. Thus, the therapist can feel that having worked towards gaining the parent's trust, s/he is now betraying them by questioning whether the care their baby receives is really good enough. This is especially strong when the parent has experienced trauma in their past, was not protected from that trauma and has intended not to repeat it with their child.

Sometimes, raising concerns does result in the parents working more closely with the therapist to break a cycle of intergenerational transmission, for example:

> A teenage mother and her mother were entangled in a situation whereby the court had determined that the baby's grandmother would be the legal guardian of the child. Initially the mother veered between battling the decision and walking away from the baby. The therapy provided a space for both adults to talk about their predicament and to join forces for the sake of the baby.

But sometimes, the parent/parents lose trust in the therapist and raising concerns – within the family and/or network – results in breakdown of the therapy. It is then challenging indeed, when rejected by the parents, to hold on to the responsibility of being the "voice of the baby" until the baby is anchored in safety by the professional network.

The therapist's role as voice of the baby is evident, too, when the risk is to the parent. Severe adult mental health issues are attended to by adult services who have variable interest in their patient as parent. When the anxiety is focused on the parent, the baby may well be forgotten. For example:

> A mother was hospitalised with paranoid convictions that her husband was abusing their baby. The father was devoted to both his wife and his baby and managed to straddle the care of both. However, in his eagerness to reunite mother and baby and the three of them as family, he tried to rush the baby's visits to her mother in hospital. The therapist discussed with father and mother what the baby may experience in meeting her mother in a state so different from her "usual one", as known by the baby. This enabled the parents to plan the reunions with the baby's age and attachment capacities and needs in mind.

We have detailed the many challenges facing practitioners working with infants and their parents. We want to conclude with a reminder to the reader of the interest and rewards this work provides. As the team of therapists at the AFC wrote in their first publication on the topic: "Babies make such good patients". Their sentience and developmental thrust align them with therapeutic efforts to support their coming "into being". Babies can bring curiosity and pleasure to relating that, with therapeutic attention, can help their parents grow into their parenthood. Conversely, as parents recover, they create the conditions in which their babies' inhibited passion and exploration can be expressed.

This field of work is also potentially rewarding to the practitioner in bringing together professional networks that may, if not for it being the perinatal period, function very separately. Adult and child mental health services, for example, often do not intersect. Nor do mental health and bio-physical/medical services. However, the perinatal period, with its intersecting of bodily and psychological factors and of adult and infant mental health, offers the opportunity for, indeed requires, multidisciplinary perspectives on health and development.

Culture too takes on a new perspective in this work. Community rites and belief systems pertaining to birth and parenting have a strong hold on new parents, and the practitioner's capacity to contribute to the wellbeing of the young family is firmly anchored in understanding their culture (Bain, Landman, Frost, Raphael-Leff, & Baradon, 2019).

Psychoanalytic parent-infant psychotherapy has brought for many a step change in their practice as therapists. In particular, learning to imagine ourselves into the world of the preverbal infant and to hold their experience in mind seems to change our very way of working. We quote Angela Joyce, a training analyst at the British Psychoanalytic Society:

> Becoming a psychoanalytic parent infant psychotherapist radically affected my practice as a psychoanalyst. I have been much more alert to the often subtle but long-lasting impact of early relational trauma that remains in the developing psyche and seeps out in so many ways. in the psychoanalysis of older children and adults these consequences become apparent and demand attention. I am much more likely to be interested in the ongoing impact of family history and the need to attend to it in all my patients. Working clinically with babies and their parents offers the opportunity to contribute to a different outcome for this next generation; to interrupt patterns that have established over at least a couple of generations.

Like MBT for children (Midgley, Ensink, Lindqvist, Malberg, & Muller, 2017), mentalizing treatment with infants in the room can offer the child's perspective in a very live way. What is special about babies is that their presence resonates with their parent/parent's experiences – emotional, visual, sensual – of their own infancy. As we know, these experiences are formative of character and object relations but are not available for conscious retrieval and reflection, or might be defensively blocked while continuing to exert their influence. Mentalizing theory strongly emphasizes the role of the imagination in thinking about both one's own and others' mental states, past and present. Having in the room an infant, parent/parents and the therapist *and* bringing to life the infant within the parent/parents and therapist can support richly imaginative, widely encompassing mentalizing perspectives.

References

Bain, K., Landman, M., Frost, K., Raphael-Leff., J., & Baradon, T. (2019). Lay counselors: Thoughts on the crossing of ecological frameworks and the use of lay counselors in the scale up of early infant mental health interventions. *Infant Mental Health Journal, 40*(3), 889–905. doi:10.1002/imhj.21814

Baradon, T. (2019). Working with the triad. In *Working with fathers in psychoanalytic parent-infant psychotherapy*. London: Routledge.

Midgley, N., Ensink, K., Lindqvist, K., Malberg, N., & Muller, N. (2017). *Mentalization-based treatment for children (MBT-C): A time-limited approach*. Washington, DC: American Psychological Association.

Raphael-Leff, J. (Ed.). (2000). *Spilt milk: Perinatal loss and breakdown*. London: Routledge.

Salomonsson, B. (2018). *Psychodynamic interventions in pregnancy and infancy: Clinical and theoretical perpsectives*. London: Routledge.

Sandler, J. (1976). Countertransference and role-responsiveness. *International Review of Psycho-Analysis, 3*, 43–47.

10 Final thoughts

We hope this book has offered the reader a largely infant-led perspective
on the vast and critical topic of the relational ties between infants and
parents. In both PPIP and mentalizing approaches, these early affective
experiences are considered foundational in shaping how an individual
mind meets other minds. We have tried to illustrate how PPIP has woven
the cloth of its theory and practice from the individual, dyadic, familial
and cultural threads that form the earliest love relationships. In so doing,
we have invited the reader to enter the experience of parent and infant in
their emotional, embodied dialogue and to consider the therapist within
this matrix. In applying mentalizing theory to infancy, we have put forward the view that the relational world that parent and infant create
forms a micro-mentalizing system in its own right. Just as each dyad or
triad has its own idiomatic subjectivity, so will each of these mentalizing
systems have its own strengths and weaknesses. One of the aspects we
have tried to emphasize is that while each relationship and mentalizing
system constitutes a world of its own, it is also closely nested within the
surrounding ecologies. We have tried to explore how mentalizing can
help this nesting of the parent-infant relationship in its social environment. We acknowledge, however, that there are circumstances, such as
communal violence and rape, under which individuals and communities
may not be able to think about the impact of the environment, including
the relational environment, on the child, and to do this, certain aspects of
the child's capacity for sentience have to be denied. It is in the context of
a safe third mind that the infant as a thinking agent can come into being;
this is a common aim of PPIP and the mentalizing approach.

In the process of discussing the topics we cover in this book, we deliberately challenged each other to clarify our thinking processes, not to
assume the contents of each other's minds, or to fall back on use of
professional terms. In other words, we tried to hold on to a mentalizing
stance but, as the theory predicts, we freely admit to occasional collapses

DOI: 10.4324/9781003024323-10

(particularly at the end of a long day). But one of the hopes that we have for this book is that in creating a dialogue between PPIP and mentalizing, we reinforce the understanding that we have a universal need to feel that we can share our emotional worlds and thinking. We consider PPIP a focussed and pre-eminent way in which vulnerable families can access this help from other minds, and we hope that this book may suggest how mentalizing and PPIP might creatively interact to continue attending to the needs of infants and their parents.

Index